DRIFTWOOD PRESS

ISSUE 9.1

EDITORS

CREDITS

Independently published by *Driftwood Press*
in the United States of America.

Fonts: Satellite, Garamond, Cinzel, League Gothic,
& Merriweather.
Cover Image & Content Illustrations: Ío Wuerich
Cover Design: Sally Franckowiak
Magazine Design: James McNulty

Published in January 2022
ISSN Print: 2578-7195
ISSN Online: 2331-7132
ISBN-13: 978-1-949065-13-8

Please visit our website at www.driftwoodpress.net
or email us at editor@driftwoodpress.net.

Table of

Contents

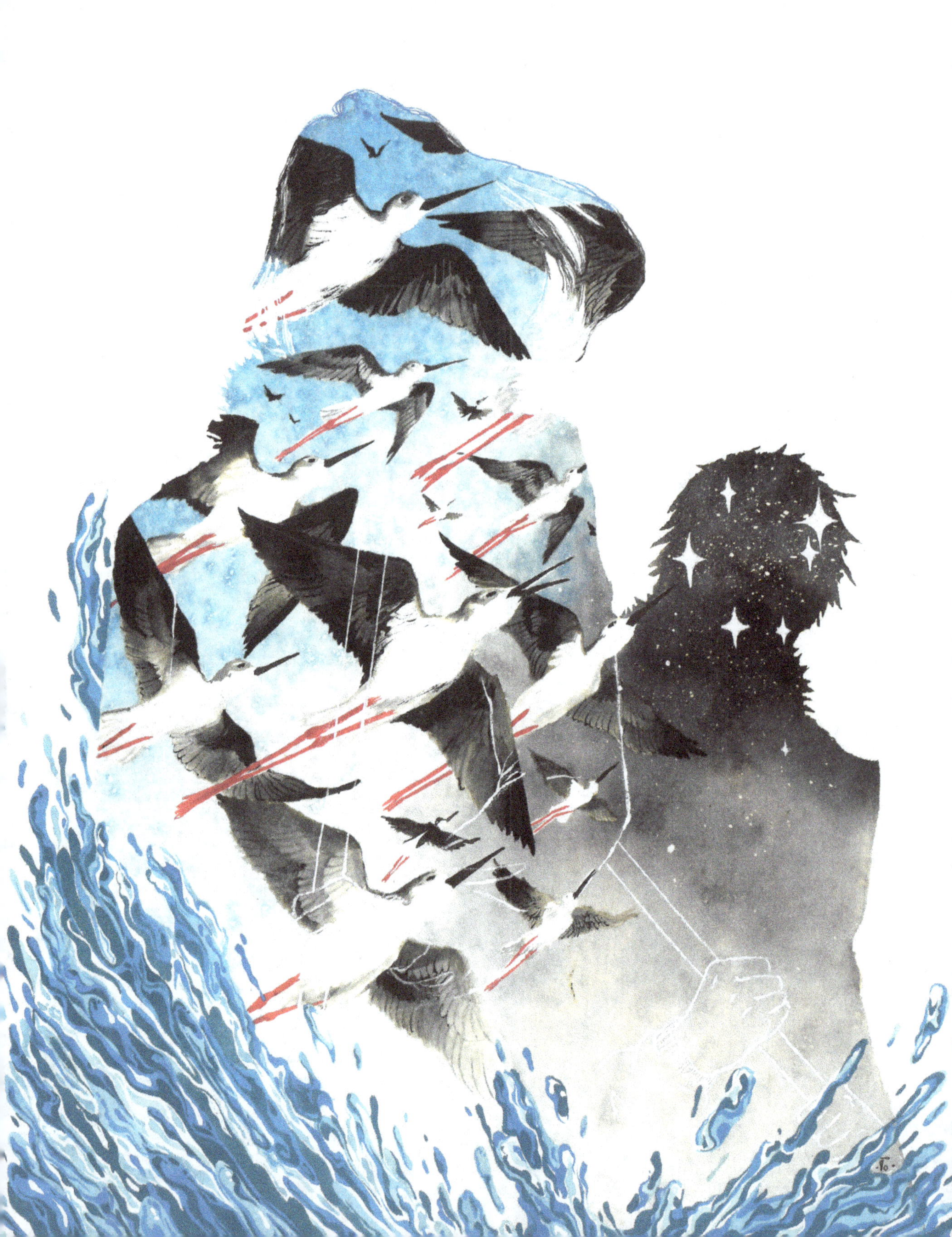

Wing Breaker

RACHEL PHILLIPPO

If I put my cheap binoculars to my eyes and look back at the shoreline, I know I will see a row of villagers, fat and furred in their coats like seals, watching my brother and I in our small kayak as we paddle away. The villagers can't see the tiny rock isle from the shore—certainly will not be able to see me set about my task—and yet they will stand watch, most of them, until I return. I picture my mother shrinking on the horizon, the damp halfmoons of her cheeks as her eyes trail my brother. Before our kayak even reaches deep waters, our father will have disappeared, leaving our mother to hold her own hand, clasped over her heart as in prayer. But I don't turn to look at them on the shore. Instead, I look forward to the vast open water, toward Bird Island, and try to keep time with my brother's rowing.

My mother said to me when I was named wing breaker, *you will do well, sunshine. It is good that you're not a nurturer.* She smiled when she said this, the skin around her eyes blossoming into a flower of creases and cracks, though she is still fairly young. She patted me proudly at the nape of the neck and seemed to breathe a sigh of relief. My mother is as much a nurturer as one can be, better than a mama fox legendary for their enormous litters, though she has only J. and me. I didn't know whether to be proud or hurt by her assessment and wondered if one can be both at once.

My brother and I are in the same boat. We call it a kayak, but it isn't really. It's a cheap, thick-plastic rowboat just big enough for two, if one of you is small. We both paddle—him on the right side, me on the left—mine a stroke and a half for his one since mine are weaker. Together, we carve a relatively straight line from our island to the crag of gray rock that constitutes Bird Island. Ahead, the sky and the water haze together into a single bright silver. Sheets of ice are beginning to melt and drift apart like the end of Pangea. It's like the start—or end—of a world every spring. We navigate around the ice sheets wordlessly. I could explain away the silence by telling myself that it's the comfort between us that needs no words, or that it's the concentration of the task that keeps our tongues still, but I would be kidding myself. The silence is an invisible force pushing between us, like a trickster spirit of old stories, or the bully wind. The wrong words wilt in my mouth, and I swallow them away.

Instead, the only sound is the cracking ice. That's not true, of course—there's the *slush* of the paddles as we pull them through the water, and the wind whistling sharply through the fine fur of my hood. There is the sound of my breath, labored already, as I push to keep time with J.'s rows. But when the ice groans it's a bone-creak crack and it drowns out everything else. It bends my heartbeat off course like standing right in the front of the speakers at town meetings, when they play the old cassette tape of our ancient songs before they begin, the drumbeat not quite in sync with my own rhythm. I draw a deep breath that freezes the insides of my nose and allow only the swiftest of glances over my shoulder. My brother sits straight-backed and strong, but there is a mechanical quality to the dip, pull, and lift of his rowing. For a moment, I wish childishly that he will lean forward in his seat, eyes alight, and tell me one of his stories like he used to do, before I could read on my own. Stories of strange and faraway places. Places with the sounds of tamarins chittering in a treetop, the chaos of thousands of people living in a single city, or my brother's favorite—of sandy beaches where they say you can hear the entire ocean in a seashell. In our village, the shells all sound the same—like the blank whiteness of the air beneath a tunnel of snow. I had loved his stories, for the magic and strangeness, but mostly for the glimmer in my brother's eyes at the telling of them. While J. always dreamed of faraway lives, I long only for the way things used to be.

I pull the paddle through the thick, icy water, working against the slight current that wants to push us back toward shore where we belong. Trying to keep a steady course toward Bird Island makes my arms ache, and I wish for the trip and the rowing to end. The island—now the size and shape of a sleeping housecat on the horizon—grows ahead of us, and my stomach tightens more with each paddle-stroke. It feels, almost, like there is a string of twine lassoed around my waist, growing tighter with each meter traveled, as though the other end of the rope is tied around our island, anchoring me back. I have the urge to look back behind me and check for that rope, but when I turn there is only my brother, grim-faced, I can tell, by the set of his chin. J., eighteen months my senior, has the male version of my own face. We have the same wide cheekbones from our mother, same dimpled chin from father. Same dark brown hair always pulled back. Although his face is covered mostly by the fur trim of his hood and the yellow-tinted glasses we must wear to make the sun's reflection off the ice and water bearable, I know he is not happy.

This is not an astute observation. The whole village knows my brother isn't happy. They know because he was wrapped prone on a sled one night and pulled by EMTs on the bright red snowmobile to the nearest hospital, two villages away, then transferred for two weeks to *Arctic Willow*: the sort of facility in which everything is made to look as peaceful as possible, yet uniformed guards watch the exits and escapes. He'd returned home two weeks ago—a month since the town had watched the emergency sled cut across the snow like a wound.

It's because of this that I've been chosen as the new wing breaker—the first female—why I'm on this boat at all, wind-whipped tears turning to ice on my lashes. I rub my face against the shoulder of my thick coat, tuck my chin into the neckline to suck some of my body heat in through my cold teeth. The task of wing breaker has long since belonged to our family, the title traditionally falling to the eldest son. It's been this way for a very long time, and I have a theory as to why. I think they offer it to the eldest son to make it look desirable, dress it up like an honor. I think our ancients were very clever this way—using ceremony to make the ugly bits of life more palatable. I guess they use ceremony the same way we use these yellow sunshades: it's a necessity here.

J. has been the wing breaker for the last two years, but not anymore. This year, since my father has no other sons, the honor is mine. It's up to me to do this successfully, not just for the village, but for my family. No one has said it outright, but I know that my mother and father are counting on me to save face, to undo what my brother has done. I could see it in the strain of my mother's smile, the too-firm grip of my father's hand on my shoulder, and the eyes of the villagers following me since the night I had been chosen—without ceremony this time—as my brother's replacement.

The wind is so sharp out on the water. Although the sunshine is beginning to melt the ice, the air temperature is freezing, and I am thankful for my coat, gloves, and boots. Outsiders in our village are incredibly rare, but I've heard of them coming with their own gear—faux-fur hoods and flimsy boots, knitted mittens—thinking they understand the cold. They leave with ermine gloves and boots rubbed with fat to keep out the water. Or, they ask to leave before the snowmobile taxi driver is even done at the tavern. Some ask us what our trick is for surviving this alien cold, or whether it is something we're born with. Neither, if you ask me. We feel the cold just the same. My fingers still stiffen in the biting wind so that twice I'm afraid I might drop the paddle and prove myself unworthy before we even reach the island. Maybe the difference is only that we have nowhere else to go.

Bird Island is near enough now that I can hear it. It's a sound I recognize. That of thousands of birds flocking in one small space, crying, crowing, singing some sort of rough grey stone song. The birds, grey-winged stilts, are dark with mottling of white. They have long, spindle-thin legs, which you can hardly believe are living appendages, and skinny spear beaks for plucking fish from the water without wetting their feathers. The stilts are fast and clever at avoiding nets. Nature had a smart design, but we villagers are smarter.

As my ears fill with the cries and crows and my heartbeat quickens, I think of the task ahead. One requirement of wing breaker is to be able to move unobtrusively among the animals. This, I can do. I will keep my heart and breathing calm, move the way my body tells me to move, without letting my brain get in the way. My brother and I have done this before.

"Do you remember the seals?" I toss my question into the wind. It seems to swirl around, buffeted among the rushing air and the distant (but growing) bird song.

But it must land at the ears of my brother, because he replies. "The pod with the cubs? Of course. I got a lashing for that one." My brother's voice is hoarse, followed by a rough chuckle, pebbles dropping into a bucket.

My rowing falters for half a beat. I'd been thinking of how once when we were little, we'd slinked our way through a pod to touch the oily, sleek new babes. I remember the exhilaration of walking among the seals, hair raised on my covered arms, smelling their wild, fishy musk, listening to the heavy breaths of the new mothers and cubs. I'd been half convinced that if I stood still and grey long enough that I'd grow flippers of my own. I hadn't remembered how my brother had refused to leave the side of one small, weak cub, the mother nowhere to be seen, or the trouble he'd gotten in when I finally got hungry enough to return home alone and our father came to collect him.

"You wanted so badly to bring home a cub."

"No, I didn't, Sunny. I just needed to know that it would be okay." His tone is gentle, even as he corrects me. As though he wishes I understood more but doesn't fault me for my ignorance.

"And the adventure was my idea, too." A familiar cold slides through my chest: a glacier flattening the air from my lungs, the wind from my sails. "I'm sorry." I redouble my rowing to veer right around a slab of ice. Sorry? Yes. But not for the trouble with the seals.

The kayak buoys slightly at the motion of his one-shouldered shrug. I don't turn around, but I can picture the gesture. "Just kids."

We are nearing the island now, and this is all we have spoken. I don't know whether my brother is angry at me for usurping his role. I don't know because I haven't asked him. The fact is, I haven't asked him anything at all since he returned home. As a sister, I am failing. I know that I am, but as much as I try to figure it out, I don't know how to do better.

I try to think like my mother. I picture her each night at dinner, how she puts aside the best cut of meat for my father who will walk in from the cold just before it's time to eat. Then the next best piece for my brother, then me, and always herself last. I picture the way, when my brother and I were young, she would chastise my brother for teasing me. Yet I could always tell, beneath that chiding, that my mother put aside her best smiles for her son. Even after he came home from *Arctic Willow*, even after we all silenced away that night, and despite our father's disapproval, my mother continued to feed my brother her sweetest smiles, her softest words. His sadness was perhaps a thing she thought she could mother away.

It takes us only an hour to reach Bird Island. It's customary for the wing breaker to have a companion to row them home, since the job is said to be physically and spiritually exhausting. However, the companion must remain on the boat. There may be only one wing breaker, because this is how it has always been done. We like to say that it's because it is a sacred and heavy task, and one of us takes the burden for the whole. But really it's because more than one person on the big rock will spook the birds too much and make a chaotic raucous. And we must be very careful to never scare the stilts away from this place where they have been roosting for centuries.

I flex my fingers as I row now, attempting to warm them up for the job ahead. There was a tool sometimes used for wing breaking in the generation before mine. Simple metal and three-pronged, you would push it open with finger and thumb, so that one long metal prong separated from the other two, insert a thin wing between the gap, and let the prongs spring back with a snap. There are a few problems with this, and the tool has largely fallen out of use. First, it's difficult to get the perfect amount of force with this sort of spring-loaded tool. Too soft a snap obviously doesn't do the job, and too hard or loud is disruptive and unnecessary. The elders and the pros all say that hands-on is best, and I have to agree. If one is going to wing break, I believe, you should have to feel the heat beneath your fingers. You should know that what you do is real.

Our boat scrapes the rough rock with a groan, and my brother and I lay our paddles long-ways inside the boat, side-by-side like two skinny bodies in a coffin. The air on Bird Island is particularly grey, a halo of bird dander lifting through the air in a haze. Scratchy, stubborn patches of greenery are thrusting long tendrils through the rock cracks. The breeze becomes wind and knocks the dander and feathers away, and then melts into a breeze again, the air thickening quickly. Yet, the stifling air is negligible compared to the sounds.

A few cries and crows rise to screeches when we are spotted. Though the birds seem mostly unperturbed, the sound still fills the air in an even more suffocating density than the dander—at ear-piercing notes—and I wonder how it's possible that they can even decipher one cousin's sound from another. But they must be communicating, as the mothers swoop and dive and glide from ground to sky to nest, miraculously not colliding in the air.

J. is standing in the boat, but he will not set foot on the island. He is not the wing breaker now. He never will be again. I step out, onto the uneven rock ground of Bird Island. We are only five feet apart, but the bird dust and scent push between us. What do I want to say to him? I want to say that I am sorry. For being chosen instead of him. No, not that. That feeling again: ice drifting across my ribcage.

"How long will it take me?" I ask.

My brother, he pulls off his glasses and his eyes are as grey as the sky and the water and rocks. He says, "I'll be waiting right here when you're done." He answers the question I meant to say, the one hiding beneath the question I ask. "I'll be here." My brother has always been this way—able to hear what's unspoken, feel the things others are feeling. This is why, I think, he is closest to our mother's heart. I know that if I reached out, and so did he, that my fingers could find his wrist underneath the mittens and seal skin. And I would feel there two still-soft long scars. And under that, a pulse almost in sync with my own. I lift my hand and wave goodbye, then I turn to the rocks and climb.

You don't really talk about the wing breaking after it's done. No one ever brags about a successful wing breaking like they do a great muskox hunt. I guess that's part of the mystique, or maybe there's just not that much to say. I know that for the two years my brother was wing breaker, he would fall very quiet for a few days afterwards. I would try to ask him questions, break into that impenetrable, important world, but he would never let me. I had thought at the time that he had wanted to keep it for himself, a prize for the oldest son. How stupid I had been.

The hike up the rocky mound is steep, but the top will soon plateau into a rough platform. I brace my hands against my knees with each heavy step, sweating beneath my coat and gloves. I want to take them off but am afraid that if I shed the layers here that I will have to drop them back down the side of the hill and risk them landing in the icy water, making for a miserable—if not dangerous—boat ride home. Some birds lay their nests in the deep crags of the hillsides, but I surpass those. It isn't necessary to find every single nest. Better to wait until I reach the top and can move through them more efficiently.

The stilts still don't seem too alarmed at my presence. I'm surprised, because these birds, though common, are usually standoffish and a little elusive. Not like the gulls that frequent the village, pillaging trash bins for fish remains. The stilts are taller, more outlandish. I keep my heart and breathing calm.

The view at the top of the mound—hundreds of birds nesting, flying, and hunting—takes my breath away. Well, that, and the ever-present wind which almost seems to be generated from the beating of so many wings in a small space. The smell is unpleasant, but the constantly moving air helps. I stop to catch my breath and slowly pull off my heavy outer layer: coat, mittens, snow pants. It feels good to be up in the air in just jeans and my long-sleeved thermal shirt. Air filtering through the tiny holes in the cotton. I'm thankful, as usual, for the rubber grip of the bottom of my boots as I pick my way over the rocks, slick with scat. At first, it's hard to see their nests, small and brown, blending into the rock and scraggly grasses. But once I know what I am looking for—a nest only slightly larger than my two cupped hands—they appear everywhere.

I walk slowly and calmly to the first nest, where there are three gaping-mouthed fledglings demanding food. I select the fattest one, and gently unfold one warm, accordion wing. If you move quickly enough, you don't even have to use your other hand to hold the bird steady. But my hands are shaking a little, and I use my left to squeeze the bird gently around the chest, tiny heartbeat thrumming unpleasantly against my palm. With my left thumb and right fingers and thumb, I press against the extended wing. Breath in and out for calm. *Give me steady hands.* Press, quick and clean, and *pop*, like a wet twig. Yes, the human hand—a miracle construction—is best for inflicting the perfect amount of force. The small bird thrashes and then stills, chest heaving in distress, and I press it back into the nest and take three hurried steps backward to watch. It shakes the injured wing, folds it back in awkwardly, and then resumes its call for food, mouth open into a wide, ridiculous diamond. I've done it. I've wing-broken before on other birds, of course, for practice. But this is the real thing. I am the first female wing breaker.

With the first wing broken, the next few nests go smoothly and my hands start to steady and I become more efficient. I'm careful to make the break quick and clean; if you are too slow, you may merely bend the soft young bones, doing more harm than good for the both of you. I choose the plumpest from each nest. With a broken wing, the babies will never be able to fly. In fact, they will never leave the nest. But these mothers, fierce tundra mothers, will not give up. They will feed and feed and feed these babies. Until they are fat adolescents, plump and soft. Long after the other babies move on, the mother birds will bring back chewed and semi-digested bits of slick mollusk, crab, and strips of pink fish meat to their broken ones, refusing to believe that they will never fly. In a few months' time, when the scabby island has grown furry patches of green, I will return and reap my harvest, sailing home with heavy bags, feathers poking from the sides of the sacks, stuffed with the meat that will feed us all well into winter. But the reaping is another job with another set of skills and traditions, and I can't think of that now. I focus on the task at hand.

By noontime, my legs are weary from picking over the rocky terrain. Some nests are built halfway obscured by rocks, and I have to ever-so-carefully shift the stones aside to get at them. Here, I must be careful not to linger, not to change too much, lest I leave my smell and presence behind. I feel sweat trickle down my spine, the direct sunlight tricking the day into thinking it is much warmer. The flex and *snap* are familiar motions to me now. So much, that I think I may wing break in my sleep well after I've finished the job and returned home. I imagine our snowy yard dotted with broken gulls and songbirds, me red-handed, and the look on my mother's face—as if the scene were sad, but inevitable.

But now the birds are onto me. I am barely a minute at each nest, but that's enough time for the adult stilts to swoop in, long beaks so sharp they pierce through the air like tiny spears. One bird dives at me, and then two. They shriek their outrage, barreling downward at impossible speed and lifting up, into an inverted bell-shaped arc, just before they hit me. Sometimes their feather tips brush my hair. And now, with only about a twenty-foot stretch of island to go, it seems the whole flock is poised to attack. My calm is dissolving into a froth of exhaustion and fear, and a dull and indistinct sadness. Against my better judgement, I pick up my heavily booted feet and run. The ground is so uneven, I should slow down, regain my composure. But the scratch of a terribly thin, clawed leg at my shoulder keeps me fleeing. The wind stings my eyes and blurs my target. I step on a rock at a slant, my right foot slipping down the rock and into a crack, just deep enough to tug at my ankle and twist. I fall long before I understand that I am falling, understanding only when my palms scrape the rock beneath me. Rolling onto my back, I see the sky above me is filled with swoops of gray.

The beat of so many wings fills your head and your chest. You never expect how loud it really is. It makes your breath hitch. I close my eyes and remind my lungs how to do their most basic function, an easy in and out. But there is something like an instinctual animal panic thrashing inside of me. What is it about the frantic flap of wings that does this? A latent evolutionary fear of some giant-winged terror? Or does the birds' own panic leak from their bodies and infest in us some sympathetic distress? A hundred wings surround me, disturbing my air, beating faster than my frantic heart. No one told me this would happen.

My ankle throbs, but not so badly that I think it's broken. Still, I crawl to the final nest, staying low to the ground and coaching my breath. The stilts, I remind myself, are not even trying to hit me. This is their scare tactic. I've seen it many times before by other birds against predators. I know this, I remind myself. I am as fierce as my tundra mother; I am the wing breaker.

The last nest cups two babies, both calling dumbly for food. The pink of the inside of their throats is like a shell, wet and pearly. Their folded-up wings are quivering at their sides. Male or female, it's impossible to tell, yet I feel that the slightly larger of the two is a brother, the smaller one his sister. They are both, yet, unbroken and new. Their dewy feathers are still plastered down to their thin skins. Late hatchlings. Despite my ankle and the hectic cyclone of diving birds, I move slowly. Or, at least, it seems that I do. I pick up the larger of the two chicks and bring the pearly shell mouth to my ear. Will it be rushing waves, or the stuffed whiteness of snow, or something else entirely?

From the shell-mouth of the larger bird I hear faintly the voice of my brother, barely audible through the *caws*. No, not from the shell-mouth, of course. J.'s voice is buoyed and pushed by the wind, up and around the rocks. He is calling, I think, to ask me if I am okay. But I can't make out his words, or even from which direction they're calling. Not over the wing-beating. I can't yell—that would distress the birds even more. And, really, he shouldn't be yelling either. He knows this. I wonder why he's calling out. Have I been up here too long? It feels like it's been minutes or days.

His voice again, but fainter. Maybe he has moved to a different side of the rock, thinking I will hear him better from another angle. Maybe he feels my distress. Or maybe he's not calling for me at all, but singing to pass the time as he waits. Maybe, unthinkably, he is paddling away. My brother, who has always wanted to be somewhere else. Me, I loved hearing the faraway stories, but always from the cocoon of my own village. It's him, always, who has really wanted to fly away.

I can't hear you, brother. But I am almost done. One wing left to break, and then I will struggle my way back down the rock. My task will be completed, the broken chicks growing fatter. One more wing, and the image of my brother being pulled away on the medic sled will finally be erased from the minds of the villagers. As though it never happened—all they will see is me: wing breaker.

The wind of the birds' wings pushes my hair and breath all around. I unfold the paper fan wing of the larger, shell-mouth chick—then stop. I settle the fat bird back in the nest, where he ruffles his downy and continues his calling. Instead, I scoop up the smaller chick. Her little sister heart is frantic and frenzied against my palm. Just one more wing to break. And then I will find J. and we will go home to our mother, who is among those waiting diligently along the shoreline, right hand clasped hard in her left. I stretch the small wing open, my hands no longer trembling. Thumb and finger poised against the tender bone. One more break, then all that is left is to wait. And to reap.

Raw Pragmatism

A Conversation with Rachel Phillippo

The following conversation was conducted by managing fiction editor James McNulty.

James McNulty: Hey, Rachel! Welcome to the pages of *Driftwood*! "Wing Breaker" is a lovely, emotional story, and I'm excited to see it in print!

Rachel Phillippo: Thank you, James! I am excited and honored. This is actually my first publication, so I feel even luckier that my story has found a great home. And *Driftwood* features such beautiful art—I can't wait to see among what images "Wing Breaker" might be nestled.

JM: Congrats on your first publication! It's always exciting to see a first-timer in fiction land on our pages every couple of years; from the editor's side, it's always fun finding a new voice.

One of our editors, Claire Agnes, said the story was "written with enough restraint that the horror avoids feeling like shallow spectacle" and "genuinely made me want to keep reading, even if with the same cold foreboding with which one drives by a car crash." I think there's a very soothing and immediately loveable voice leading the piece, one which smoothly leads you through that "horror" and "foreboding" of the back half of the story. Could you talk a little about finding the voice of this character?

RP: Yes! So, this protagonist is very pragmatic. She gets right to business and gets things done—in this way she is a better match for the role of wing breaker than her brother ever was. I wanted her to be someone the reader could trust to be really forthright and honest in her telling of the wing breaking, without falling into melodrama. It was really interesting and fun to write her voice, because in some ways she's so unlike myself—whereas I tend to overthink most situations, here I had to pull back and let Sunny tell it more straightforward. I think we all sort of have those two dueling voices in our heads—one logical, one emotional—always sort of teeter-tottering for balance. In the case of Sunny, I wanted the logical side to be her dominant voice. I think her drive to prove herself and to solve problems (for herself and for her family) makes her really likeable, despite her flawed inability to be there emotionally for her brother.

JM: What revision work went into the voice, if any? She reads so smoothly, and there's so much pathos in the voice from the get-go. You keep it emotional without ever getting too sentimental or melodramatic. How do you strike this balance?

RP: "Wing Breaker," like many of my stories, began with a voice and an image. I knew I'd have a young woman acting as wing breaker, and her voice was one of the first aspects of the story to arise, really driving the plot and development of the adventure from there. Which is why, I think, in the original draft that you read there was a lot of direct address and more monologuing—I was both cultivating the voice and using it to set the tone of the story. Then, of course, you helped me to pare back on that over rounds of revisions—getting to the point now where the voice is fundamental but not distracting. I appreciate all of your insight there and the push to get this story from promising to publication-ready.

As for striking a balance between emotion and sentimentality: I do think that simply the nature of this protagonist is useful here—her pragmatism. But beyond that, avoiding melodrama is something that I do try to be mindful of. I do a lot of writing about motherhood, and I think it is important to write about motherhood in a way that is not just honest and emotional, but also raw—not romanticized or overly sentimental as can easily be the pitfall. So that is something frequently in the back of my mind. In this case, giving Sunny a very tangible goal with real-life consequences provides a helpful balance to the emotional aspect of the story.

JM: I think many writers share the same tact: overwriting the interior to get into the character and story, then having to go back and cut away at the excess. Since there isn't much dialogue in this story, so much of Sunny's voice comes through interiority. We spoke a good bit during revisions about the interiority that opens the story; I know you trimmed a good bit and only the strongest remain, punctuated now by description and actions to keep us grounded in the exterior world. There's an argument to be made that opening with this interior strongly endears us to the character—especially when the interior is as well-written and has such a strong voice as here—but of course it also slows the story's momentum. What do you think about this trade off?

RP: It may make you laugh (or weep) to hear that "Wing Breaker" is actually a fairly fast-paced story for me. But I certainly see your point—starting off a story this slowly is probably a risky move. Personally, though, as a reader I am willing to follow an interesting and well-written character just about anywhere—washing the dishes, taking a stroll. If the character is likeable and dynamic, then I'm up for it. I guess all that is to say, I enjoy a very character-driven story. That being said, there has to be a payoff. There needs to be something at stake for the character, and the ending should be impactful to both the character and the reader. Sometimes I think the stories with a slow burn end up having the greatest payoffs. I hope I accomplish that here with the final scene.

JM: Certainly we thought the payoff worked, and I agree with your comments on slow burns; I'm betting many of our readers will feel the same. I want to circle back around to something you mentioned earlier. For most writers, writing something that is "honest and emotional" leads to sentimentality and melodrama. If I'm following correctly, you said the practicality of the character (I love her line about rituals only being a way to glam up something ugly) helped to temper that emotion—alongside her tangible goal. Do you have any other tips for avoiding honest writing turning into sentimental writing?

RP: I think simply how our characters react to emotion is a factor in avoiding melodrama. Which is another element I appreciate you helping me to fine-tune in this story, James. Our characters can (probably should) feel emotion strongly: they can show the emotion through their actions, they can even directly examine and mull over that emotion if needed—but they don't necessarily need to be able to name (or even understand) it. I think sometimes we make the mistake of allowing our characters to be too self-aware, and they're maybe able to remove that emotion from themselves and think too directly about it, leading to melodrama. That's neither realistic (for most of us), or all that interesting, right? There's a tension created when the reader is able to understand more about a character's motivations than the character does himself. Basically, it comes down to showing versus telling.

Another way to avoid sentimentality, I find, is just to be mindful of word choice. I mentioned I write a lot about mothers and daughters: if a mother is regarding her new baby, likening her newborn complexion to a pink rose petal, this is probably cliché and sentimental. If, instead, the mother thinks the baby's skin has the pearlescent pink sheen of new skin grown after a wound... Well, that's less expected and certainly less "precious."

JM: All of this makes perfect sense to me, though I don't remember there being much melodrama even in early drafts of "Wing Breaker." So often, even the most complex of issues in writing, when boiled down, become different forms of that tell versus show issue; it's often regarded as a rookie issue, but I think even veteran writers sometimes struggle with it—though perhaps their articulations of the problems become more nuanced. I think you also make a very good point about what the reader should understand versus what the character should understand; it's easy for writers to forget that these two things are not synonymous.

You mentioned earlier how the story began with a voice and an image. What inspired the voice and image of "Wing Breaker"?

RP: I've always been very interested (as I'd hazard a guess most writers and readers are) in anthropology and different ways of living around the globe. When I was a kid, my dad would often tell me the abridged version of articles he had read or shows he had seen about interesting groups of people. One that stuck in my mind and grew in my imagination over the years was of a group of real people who (at one point) practiced a form of "wing breaking," probably bearing very little resemblance to the process in my story. But it was this kernel of memory that took root in my imagination. The final scene in "Wing Breaker," with Sunny on Bird Island, is the fictionalized image that had formed in my mind, taking on a life of its own. I never really gave thought beforehand to what the voice might be like, or really who the character was; she just seemed to grow right alongside that image I had been carrying around. So when I sat down to write the story, deciding to begin on the boat, it was Sunny's voice who started telling the story. Of course later you have the fine-tuning of the voice, the considerations about motive, etc. But oftentimes for me, I have the image and the voice, and the question from there is what's actually going to happen.

JM: And how'd you progress from there?

RP: I sat down each morning with a rule for myself that I would write for an hour, regardless of whether I ended up being able to keep anything I wrote. That allowed me to be a little less anxious about not knowing what was actually going to happen. I knew that I would begin the story on the boat, and the goal was to make it to Bird Island. Having a specific physical task for my character to complete was very helpful for me. I really enjoyed writing the physical actions and movements of the whole adventure. From there, the external challenges helped me drive the story forward, and I worked on trying to strike a balance between those outward struggles and her internal conflicts.

JM: You mention writing an hour a day. Just out of curiosity, about how many days did it take to write the first draft? Then how much time went into revision before submission? I think many writers don't quite know how much time they should be spending on the drafts before submission, so maybe you can help give them a sense.

RP: It's been four or five years since I first sat down to write "Wing Breaker," and I didn't keep a record of my daily progress (although come to think of it, that's a great idea). But I'd estimate that first draft took me a week or two. Which maybe sounds slow given the length of the story, but there were ultimately sections that ended up deleted at the end of the hour, or some days in which I took some time rewriting previous sections to get back into the voice and feel of the story. By the time I submitted this story to *Driftwood*, it had already been through a few rounds of my own surface-level revision, as well as reviewed by a mentor from the MFA program I was completing at the time. For me, it is often helpful to put a story away for a little while (whatever that means to you—a few days, a week, months) between revision rounds. This allows me to look at the story with less attachment and see the flaws more clearly. It took several drafts and lots of changes before I felt ready to send it out into the world.

JM: Outside of your father's role in the premise, what role did research play?

RP: I was actually intentional about not researching for this story. I really wanted to make sure what I was writing was complete fiction and not loosely based on any real culture—I didn't want to get too wrapped up in sticking to factual logistics or trying to accurately represent any group of people. I did do some research on the birds, though, in order to classify these fictional Bird Island creatures as part of the "stilts" family. Everything else is imagined.

JM: Were you able to find the clipping your father gave you all those years ago? It would be curious and fun to find out about the real story behind wing breaking. We've published stories on both sides of this debate: stories that were painstakingly researched and specific (I'm thinking of Mason Boyles' "Myopic" in issue 8.1) as well as stories like yours where the writer preferred creativity to research. Talk to me a little more about the pros and cons of each, to your mind. Are you going to stick with this method in the future, or will certain stories demand research?

RP: I've actually asked my dad about this, and he thinks that it may not have been an article at all—but an old David Attenborough series from the 80s! Unfortunately, I've yet to find the episode. I would love to watch it now and see how far my wing breaking imaginings stray from reality. Now that the story is "done" (as done as writing ever is), I will likely go back and do the research. I actually love research, and find that collecting ideas—usually from the natural world—can lead to a lot of neat, enriching details and ideas. I typically do some reading in regards to wildlife, often insects, that appear in my stories. Sometimes the truth is stranger than fiction and will spark new themes. Plus, I want to make sure I get my facts right. That being said, I do tend to shy away from being very specific when it comes to locations and groups of people. I don't like to feel constricted by the need to accurately portray a certain town, for example. I like to be free to build my world in a way that suits my story, rather than building my story around the world. But I imagine plenty of writers work in exactly the opposite direction with great success.

JM: Talk to me about the structuring decisions in "Wing Breaker." I thought it was a wise move to hold the description of the ritual until midway through the story. We're traveling for so long with her—and a sort of foreboding feeling—before we're told about the ritual she's been hinting at. There's good build-up before you give away the reveal.

RP: She may not buy into the ceremony and superstition of the ritual, but I still wanted to build up a certain mystique around it before the reveal. Also, delaying the description prompts the reader to instead pay attention to Sunny in the beginning of the story. Rather than focusing on the wing breaking, the reader has time to get a good sense of her character and her conflict with her brother (and herself) before we reach that point. This isn't something I necessarily planned when I sat down to write. More like, it is what felt natural to the story right from the get-go. Then, of course, you get to revisions and have to think about pacing and structure. Which is where you helped me to pare down the beginning, getting to that reveal a little bit faster as a result. The final scene was always the endgame—I was always working toward that point on Bird Island with the final wings. So in my mind, the whole story was a big setup for this scene. Which I suppose is probably the goal in every slow-burning short story, but I was perhaps particularly conscious of it.

JM: What writers have influenced your writing—and specifically "Wing Breaker"—the most?

RP: I enjoy stories with elements of magical realism and just general strangeness. Over the course of grad school I read a lot of Kelly Link, Karen Russell, and Lorrie Moore. I think we all have a handful of influential stories that are always sort of in the backs of our minds. For me, a couple of those would be "Stone Animals" by Kelly Link, "The Ceiling" by Kevin Brockmeier, "Terrific Mother" by Lorrie Moore, and "Tower of Babylon" by Ted Chiang.

JM: What other mediums have influenced your work? How?

RP: When it comes to other literary genres, all of the YA and science fiction novels I enjoyed reading growing up affected how I use character voice, as well as my desire to bring a sense of adventure to a story whenever possible. As far as other mediums go, music has certainly been influential to me. I didn't listen to any music at all while working on "Wing Breaker," probably because sounds are such an important element to this story and I wanted to be attentive to those. But while working on other projects (and definitely when I'm in more of the planning and daydreaming phase than physically writing) I will often listen to music that puts me in mind of a place, or character, or just emotion that connects me to that story. I do spend the most time thinking about stories (and sometimes even writing them) outdoors. I like to be close to the natural world when possible, and a lot of my stories' action occurs outside—be it crossing icy waters or chasing a whitetail through a cornfield. Can gardening count can as an artistic medium? I do some of my best thinking and organizing of thought while pulling weeds and picking zucchinis.

JM: I know many folks who would consider it one, yes. Gardening is certainly its own skillset; I've killed two bonsai in the past year—hopefully you're better at it! I also noticed the YA influence in "Wing Breaker"; there's a distinct "YA interiority voice" that your writing here shares. YA writers are often very good at nailing that smooth, natural, innocent voice.

RP: Thank you! Sunny is a young character, so her age combined with her somewhat simple view of the world lends well to that YA style of voice. And I totally agree with your point about YA writers—I think their mastery of voice is one of the things that makes YA literature so enjoyable to read.

JM: Now that "Wing Breaker" is finished, what are you working on next?

RP: I plan to first go back and take a close look at other stories I've written—primarily about women in the Midwest—and work on revising those and getting them ready for submission. I feel more confident doing this having worked with you on "Wing Breaker." I've also been working on a project with my dad and brother in which we each write the perspective of a different character, the goal being to interweave their three arcs into something like a novella. That has been a really interesting and somewhat complicated venture. And I think there is definitely a young adult novel in my future, though I couldn't tell you when!

JM: I think your writing style will work very well for a YA book, but I'll be most excited to read the stories about women in the Midwest; let me know when they're published!

Is there anything else you'd like to mention in particular—about writing or "Wing Breaker"?

RP: Thank you, I certainly will! And for any other new or aspiring writers out there, I'd like to encourage you to just go for it. As I mentioned earlier on, this is my first publication and I've really just started working on getting my stories out into the world. I know convincing yourself that your work is good enough can be a big mental hurdle. Write what interests you and it will speak to others, too.

JM: Thanks so much for taking the time to speak with us, Rachel! "Wing Breaker" is a lovely story, and I'm excited to see what you write in the future!

RP: Thanks so much, James! I couldn't be more excited to have "Wing Breaker" find a home in *Driftwood.* And to everyone else—happy reading!

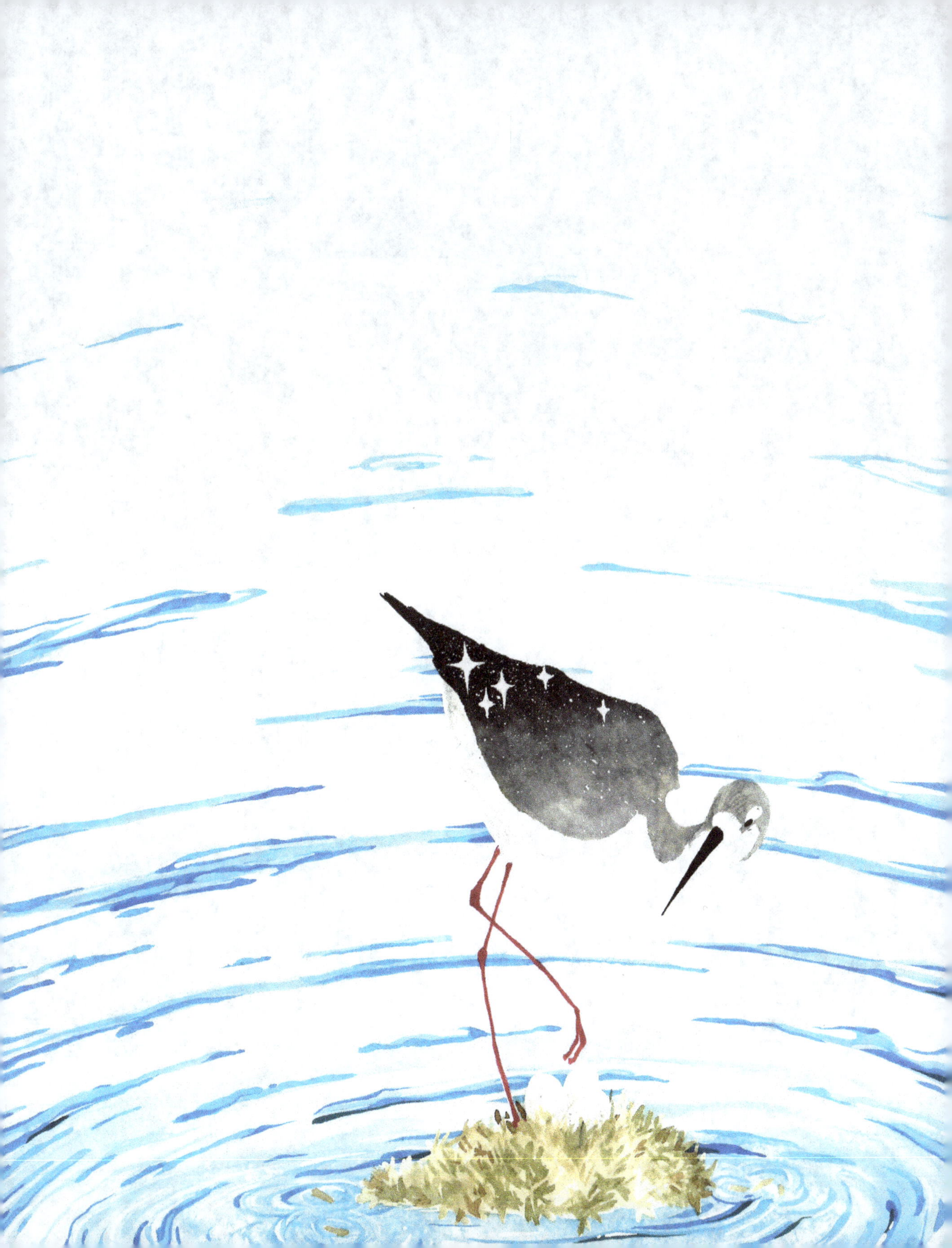

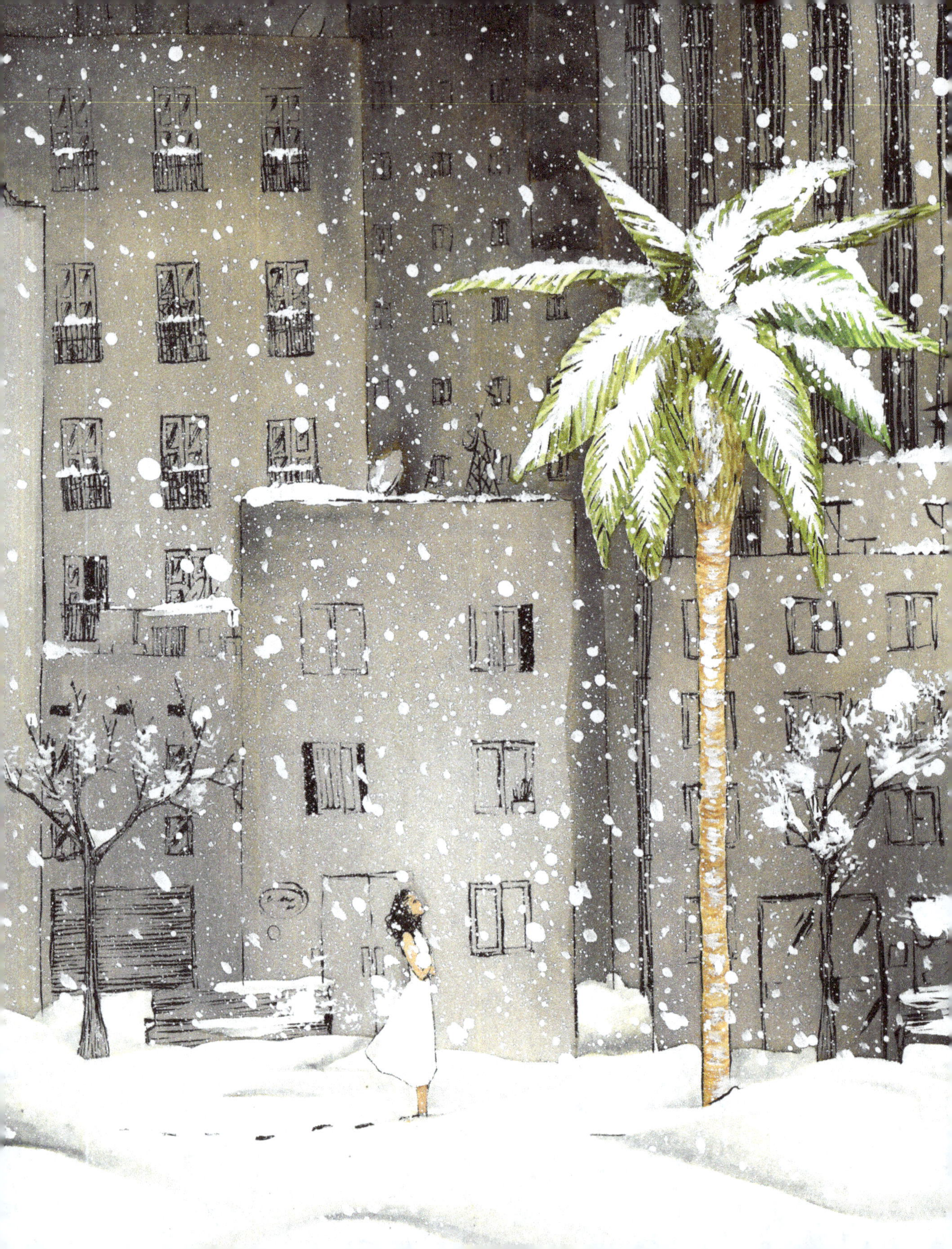

SPANISH SOAP OPERAS KILLED MY MOTHER

DAILIHANA ALFONSECA

I. Island Gal

There used to be more fat between the Earth and my bones. Back when the palm trees swayed our family to sleep in hammocks made of plantain leaves. Way back when our homes had no glass on the windows, the air smelled vibrant and green, the walls rough with concrete like sea foam and salt water. Iguanas would climb into bed with us at night to whisper stories of our ancestors in our ears, messages all three of us needed to hear. My mother had already let the man come in. Domesticate her tongue and now she screamed and ran whenever the iguana tried to warn her of the plans of God.

I barely remember my father. Yet I remember he links me to the Oyo Empire. The only memory I recall with him nauseates me in sweet pink and sticky sap. Strawberry sickness covers the dashboard now. He is upset. I cry. He laughs. His gold chains in the Caribbean sun glint at me and trap their way into my soul. I didn't know then what I know now. About the paging of addicts needing their fix or why his fingers glistened with jewels and money that came from a war that began in opium dens to the east. All I know is that I am a glutton for excess because of him. He teaches me my first lesson. Too much of anything can only result in sickness and in death.

I remember how Mami chased Papi around with a bat after she found him bringing us home with the lady who had the same color hair as her but not her height. The cherry red lips of his convertible busted open as she drove the bat into his car like the cigarette gently sitting on his bottom lip. While Mami chases Papi, I see Papi chasing other women.

"Do you think he feels bad?" The gum snaps between the question and the clucking of hens in the yard. My mother's wrist now laden with my father's spoils scrapes the white grains from a bottom-heavy pot. "No, men never feel bad for anything." The *pastelito* with its cumin, *sazon*, and ground beef screams at her from the frying pan. It yells the sizzling protest of my virility and misunderstanding. Our small house, hot with tension as Mami waits up for his arrival and when my father does not come home she thinks it is just another woman. After his death our island stinks fragrantly of deceased sorrow as we board an avian boat towards the broken sea of opportunity.

We arrive with one suitcase and no English to our name. My grandmother is already in the mainland of success. Abuela is not as domineering as Mami makes her seem. Abuela's love is stern and gently embracing, it holds us in between the French bread she slathers in butter and dips in her cafe con leche. She is sick but cannot see it yet. She places us in front of the telenovelas. We learn that Spanish women are sultry, and sexy, and dramatic, and loud, and crazy. We learn that life is full of drama and chaos and struggle and pain. We learn that women behave like flies caught in the web of men and money. Wriggling in skirts, and heels, and eyeshadow only to further fasten our fate and be devoured by phallic ruthlessness.

II. NewYoricana

"*¡Mami, mira!*" I point at the pigeon on the fire escape of my grandmother's one-bedroom American dream. Three daughters, two mothers, one family.

"Berry nice-ee," Mami says without looking out the window. The screen with the telenovelas hypnotize her further.

My sister and I hover and ask questions that bother her. We play too loudly and we run too quickly and we are not welcome here. America is not like our island of *coqui* calls and tropical echoes. Here, we are always inside and quiet, the only green the philodendron within the hanging basket under my grandmother's eyes—not like our island where the dirt touched the mud touched our souls. Instead it is the snow which touches me here in this vast space full of fluorescent sadness.

At night Mami dresses and heads towards the places that make her feel like the women in the telenovelas. Our grandmother watches over us as the city of New York swallows Mami's soul. Just like the characters she idolizes on the bright neon screen of possibilities.

My tongue too fat inside my mouth. Words too slick for my tongue. My tongue, with its heavy R's and soft Y's. With its sticky papaya P's and sizzling salami S's. Two islands on my tongue. Two Islands on my tongue.

Mami cries all the time now. She yells all the time now. She's sick all the time now. The walls are always white, and the sky is always grey, and the birds always honk, and the parrots always blast their songs of pain and agony in the early morning Bronx bachata. But still she goes out. The men, they holler and they praise but they never stay. A product of 90s disco and New York grime. The white lines on the table hide her face like the bars on our confinement. The iguanas cannot, will not, come inside anymore. I am throwing rocks at them, hoping they'll disappear with my tongue's heavy accent. And soon we move away from *abuelita* because Mami cannot stand her Castilian composure.

It was always cold here and it has always been cold to me. Like the cruel lady stepmother who does not want my glass slipper to fit. I pine at the lives on the screen now too. Remembering when mothers where mothers like Mami.

"Hey, Spic!" I look at the boy and am puzzled. His eyes the same color of the water in my soul. Clear and green and blue and seeing me. He is the same toasted coconut of my mother and grandmother and my cousins. Unlike my sister and I who are like *Brugal*, mixed and aged and made into rum.

I smile. "My name no Spic. Es—"

Cutting me off, he spits in my face. "You and your dirty sister don't belong on this side of the street." He pushes me into the reality of the gutters. His olive skin the base toxicity of a race we never asked to be a part of. "No spic English, no spic English." He sings and laughs. He laughs and sings. Then starts to skip down towards the store where both our mothers buy oregano, tomatoes, and garlic.

In this city the hurricanes call out to me as they give me their great flood and wash away the boy in a rage during the gales of March.

III. Pilgrim

We live someplace colder now—a place where immigrants landed just like us. Mami's body begins to whither in the wintry embrace of her illness. Yet she continues her fairytale and hides her expiration date. She flees again, leaving the iguanas to cross the oceans, highways, and certain death for her. Soon, abuelita is dead. There is no more yelling on the phone about how hecha y derecha she is. She has no one to explain her freedoms and liberties to. Gone is the great matriarchal Hope. Esperanza is no more. I am no one here except the girl who came from the place we all came from.

"You weren't born here?" My classmate's eyes look at me as if I am some other version of myself. "But your English is...*good.* Not just good, it is *great.*" His parent's accent still heavy on his tongue even though he was born here and I not.

In this new place I beam with pride. I no longer possess the tongue of *mar y sol.* I am now a real *Americana* just like the girls in the Lifetime telenovelas who overcome and make it to Harvard. "That will be me one day," I say. Spring has awakened me.

We were all on the school bus the first time I was introduced to the rules of Adam. To the power allowed Lillith but not Eve. Boys gave me the key to womanhood and I was now an Americana who rolled up her skirt when she got on the school bus and put on the lip gloss she hid in a pencil case and shaved her legs without permission.

"*Chacho, nena, pero que greña.*" The beautician looks at my head in disgust.

We are sitting in the salon learning that all men lie and cheat and that all women suffer. The rollers on my head smell like acrylic, Tommy girl, and the humid smoke of hair fighting to maintain its crimp while the heating tools repress it into conformity. Into perfect suburban homes with manicured lawns and two cars in the driveway who come home from real jobs. Just like the girls on Walt's channel and that of five-cent movie theaters. I should wait to put on mascara and shave my legs, but I don't. Instead I idolize a freedom I see in the American girls. I am an American girl with a *campesina* mother who still speaks like a *spic.* Her tongue heavy with *arroz con guandules* and the food I hate that she makes. I hate her and how she reminds me of the boy who threw me into the gutter. She brings me shame. I am always angry now. Silenced and obedient but violently and savagely angry. I rebel against the iguanas' warnings. I hate them too.

I flee in the early morning light. A Honda Accord and two boys who know no better. When mothers tried the best they could without the fathers who created these Victor-like creatures. They are hidden in forests of excuses brought out of hiding with bills made of pitchforks, American streets dressed as prosperity, and the result of mobbish poverty.

I beg Mami to leave him, to choose her children over this man, but her response is that I am not the master of her fate and destiny. And in this light and in that temperature I feel abandoned, although it is I who fled this time. I did not understand the life of a single mother who puts up with men to feed her children. I did not see the bruises underneath the cellulose makeup of her skin, of her body. I am no longer a child, I decide, when the whisper arrives in the breeze and I grab the hand of the first stranger the tumble weeds drag towards me.

That boy with green hair and blonde eyes. Made me scrub my father so that his skin marbled under me into the cold flesh of paper and ink. All so I could fit into his pockets and his bible. So I could stay between the sheets of privilege and power. I scrubbed as much of my island and beauty and untame into consent. For survival was all at his mercy and command. While I was with him no one looked twice unless it was dark.

We pull into a desolate park. The park's bones an echo of a wealthier cousin in a community not abandoned by fathers.

"You better not bitch out." The boy pulls his penis out.

His friends stand outside, their backs to the car and the smell of cigarettes and maryjane wafting in through the splintered window, stabbing me with insecurity. This boy's ride had seemed like a sanctuary. Yet now I am trapped. I must follow through or else I know not where I am or what I am going to do. How could I, a girl of only sixteen, tell these boys of only sixteen that I was afraid and cold and alone. When we are all just playing adult. If escape had meant this truth, then every escape I encounter in life will only be a thunderstorm.

The indigo blue textile of back-bending labor and cerulean residue of bondage and conquest. Immigrant ants. Ancestor Copy Cats. All of us. Tainos, Yoruba, Mayans, Aztecs. Pagans, Celtics, and Saxons alike. And all the other ancient places I went to that summer are scarred and pillaged and colonized by polytheistic deserters.

I lived in this way for many moons and suns, a premature sapling in an open field. I floated, rustled, trickled over the city of Boston, and some days I still feel the city pummeling into me during my dreams. I search in her structure for memories of me. All that stares back are the empty alleys I desperately try to forget. I am convinced there is not enough space in my mouth for all these dialects and languages. I spit out accents and osmosis. I am no more the girl from DR and PR. I am now a girl from the US and not the islands on my tongue.

I trek, and trudge, and march through more of the city's crevices, finding crumbs of generosity. And then Mami calls. To shame and guilt and lure me back to her hovel of weakness. No more. No shame, pain and Cain in, within, me. I will no longer be the article of her scheme. As she pleads on the other end of the line, I simper at her distress. The would-be truths that lay behind my eyes reflect the lies she lets inside: that she is both worthless and invisible.

The man with the car kept me the safest. He did not even pick me up or shake me to see what gifts would be allowed him for the Yule, and yet I still gave him the economy of my soul. This man's garden was two bedrooms wide and a television screen long. And I was on his Insula Canaria in his garden of haram. He kept me a resident above two islands next to more islands under three. I am no longer the honored ivy league hopeful. Instead I have begun to idolize the women in the screen just as my mother before me.

Strength is in the space between my ears, unmarred by the hand of Adam and untouched by the rape of Eve's metra.

IV. Expirer

Mami was sick when I returned. She progressed back to her beginning. The beginning where she sank down into the sky. Here, the roots come into her and grab her ribs and turn her into a large palm tree. And now the iguanas speak for she. They climb and lay in her leaves and rustle her awake when I come home. They whisper to me and now I hear them calling me home in the winds and crashing waves of Salisbury Beach.

"*¡Todo pesto fue tu culpa!*" The phone vibrates from the strength of my mother's sister's voice, "*¡La Mataste!*"

"Here, take this." I hand the phone to my younger sister and walk outside. Looking up at the night sky,

I begin to count the stars.

"Hey, are you okay?" My uncle, Hebel, sits down beside me.

"She says I killed her." I undulate on the patio swing. "Do you think that's true?"

Hebel gives a deep sigh and looks up at the sky with me. "Do you think it's true?" He turns towards me and watches me intently—more than likely making sure I do not fall prey to my anxious retaliations to life.

"I think the soap operas killed Mami." I look at him, and he stares at me as if I have three heads.

Telenovela

A Conversation with Dailihana Alfonseca

The following conversation was conducted by managing fiction editor James McNulty.

James McNulty: Hey, Dailihana! Our editorial team loved the lyricism, structuring, themes, and purposeful compression present in "Spanish Soap Operas Killed My Mother." I can't wait to see it in our pages soon.

Dailihana Alfonseca: Hi, James! Thanks to you and the editorial team for seeing such validity in the work. I'm so grateful that the lyricism, structure, and movement of the text spoke to you and the editors. I'm also very excited for it to be read and experienced within the pages of *Driftwood Press*.

JM: This is such a compressed story—so much going on in its few, short pages. There's so much to talk about! Well, let's start with the structuring—of which the purposeful compression I mentioned earlier is a critical part of.

Formally, the story swaps between two modes (italics and non-italics), many somewhat episodic vignettes, and four distinctive sections. There's a ton going on structurally, visually, and formally here. Do you have a background as a poet? What influenced this structure, and why did you decide to tell the story in the form that you have here?

DA: While it may seem natural due to the story, I do not have a background as a poet. Surprisingly enough, after getting my business undergrad, I began my foray back to the world of literature as an aspiring children's writer. It was not until I took a creative writing class with Dr. Landon Houle, author of *Living Things*, that I found my poetic agency and rhythm. This story initially began as a modular experiment in her class and became what you are reading today.

The italicized and non-italicized differences initially began with how I read the story to myself. Certain parts I'd read in my head and other sections I would read out loud. Once I realized I was writing a story based around how this specific type of media affects the livelihood of my character and their surroundings, I decided to make each section like an episode inside of a series just like a telenovela (aka a Spanish soap opera). Telenovelas were prominent in my household as I grew up and every episode was full of drama, intrigue, and twists. Our surroundings genuinely became like these characters and their lives in some ways—and not always positively.

My story relies on some of those same tumultuous methods and literary movements to captivate and create imagery that divulges how the character experiences self-discovery within each setting. In between the character development within telenovelas, you'll see there is a lot of backstory that many viewers become privy to through the use of voice over, and it's used to grasp the intentions, inner thoughts, and developing ideas of the characters as they progress within the storyline. What began almost accidentally became intentional and this story morphed into adapting this same exercise as kind of bridge between the characters inner dialogue and the surroundings being experienced. However, instead of narrating how my character is plotting the downfall of their nemesis, the italicized areas transition the reader from inside the character's mind to outside of the character's body.

JM: What a lovely explanation! Modeling the story off the format of another medium sounds like a great experiment, and I'm glad it worked out so well for you here! *General Hospital* played in my house often while I was growing up; it's not quite the same as a telenovela—but similar. Do you know much about American soap operas? For readers who don't know much about telenovelas and how they differ, how would you describe that type of program?

The telenovela structuring explains the episodic nature and the italicized portions, but what about the four segment breaks, each noting the character's development toward Americanization & homogenization? How'd you land on incorporating those? Clearly, we think your multi-level structuring worked, but I imagine a lesser writer would muck it up—the contents becoming *too* confusing and scattered, too messy.

DA: I am not an expert of any kind on soap operas and it has been years since I sat down and let myself be engulfed by it all. However, I heard American soaps go on for years. That is one of the most distinct differences I have come across. Another difference is that Spanish soap operas also tend to be more condensed and fast paced as a result of only lasting a few seasons.

The segment breaks were something I recently added to the story and came about as a result of looking at it with "fresh eyes." Once I took a break and came back to it, I began to work on this idea that each transition should reflect where the character is physically and in life. There actually were two more "chapters" in there, but I ended up taking them out and keeping it as condensed as the life of telenovelas on the networks I grew up watching. Whenever I visit my elderly relatives and their TV is turned to *Telemundo* or *Univision*, there is always a commercial announcing either the end or the beginning of another story. I wanted my story to reflect upheaval as drama and growth as the twisting limbs that help guide us as we learn who we are in places that are often not very kind, warm, or welcoming. In this way it reflects where the character is and how she is developing past one identity and towards another, specifically those identities impressed upon her as a result of migratory instability.

JM: What was in the two chapters that you cut?

DA: If I tell you that those two chapters have now begun developing into a new story would you let me be vague? Honestly, it was a part of the story that needed more development, and since this is technically a short story, I did not want to leave too much to answer towards the end. So I kept them to myself to work through.

JM: You mention the story's themes of identity—those identities impressed on a migrant child by American sociological pressures. The story seems pessimistic in this respect. Three quarters in, the speaker has almost entirely disavowed her homeland, her original culture. "I am now a girl from the US and not the islands on my tongue." By the end of the third section, she's "begun to idolize the women in the screen just as [her] mother before [her]." This seems to—optimistically—imply that she can't escape her heritage, try as she might. But perhaps the most elusive moment is the final titular line: "I think the soap operas killed Mami." To the mostly Americanized protagonist, the mother's continuous embrace of her original heritage while she was displaced caused her death; the mother didn't forsake her heritage as the speaker did. Or at least, that's how I read it. How do you understand this line?

DA: Whoa. Loaded question. Okay, well, first, I write about the experiences I have seen or have known myself. From that standpoint, I would argue that the layered disownment of heritage is presented so as to highlight the grappling of one's own self and the impressed self being absorbed through cultural osmosis.

The impressed self here, represents the identity one uses in the real world, so to speak. Cultural osmosis, therefore, is the learned patterns, behaviors, or biases we exhibit physically, psychologically, and emotionally which are a result of how (and sometimes where) we are raised.

I wanted to shed light on how many immigrants culturally assimilate and disavow their customs as a result of negative cultural trauma. I attempted to make the interactions a part of the development so as to show how the many identities the protagonist is grappling with reflect off how she views herself and experiences her own agency, body, and life as someone who is growing up in America but does not see herself as "American." Since I can only speak from personal experience, I know and have seen many immigrants, who are proud of where they come from, yet abandon accents and cultural anchors out of survival—something I felt was pivotal to showing the "old school" way our grandparents and great-grandparents dealt with worse cultural traumatic conditions, and what this taught us about survival in America.

Second, while it may seem that the protagonist is "forsaking" her heritage, what she is in fact forsaking are the cultural barriers that constrict her in the eyes of society. The occidental world is a complex, layered beast of cultural ideals that may feel alienating to the immigrant identity and which create a void between the perceived self and the "you" perceived by the society one exists within. Heavily perpetuated and often dramatized racial stereotypes and prejudices continue to be impressed on our society regularly through movies, TV shows, and now digital platforms. This continues to create a division within societies every day—and not simply within one's self. The television is a mode within the story and stands as the envoy of societal pressures as well as the ideals of self and the projection of cultural identity. It may seem that she is mistakenly forsaking her heritage; however, what the character attempts to forsake are the oppressive mental shackles that continue to be perpetuated whether or not she watches the same television show that her mother does. The realization that soap operas killed her mother at the end, is in fact a moment of enlightenment. It is a realization that this particular type of media causes this particular type of demise. That is the most powerful statement within the entire story, I feel like.

JM: Interesting! It seems I had a somewhat different interpretation from the one intended by the author. To my mind, either reading works well enough and communicates the general ideas. This is both a benefit and negative of more loose, poetic writing: some finer points may be lost or misinterpreted in the spare style, but the general ideas come through and a reader's own identity and knowledge base plays a part in their interpretation. I'll be curious to see how our readers interpret the story alongside your explanation above.

Is there anything else you'd like to say on this topic of migrant identity—as it relates to "Spanish Soap Operas"? You mentioned another story on the way—is this topic the primary focus of your writing at this time?

DA: I find that to be the most fascinating fact about art. Regardless of artistic form of delivery, the work can be interpreted and understood in different ways. I am excited to share the story and can't wait for readers to engage with rhythms within the text.

In relation to "Spanish Soap Operas Killed My Mother," I hope the story helps shed light on lesser explored migrant identities within our communities, specifically that of women and girls. While each migrant experience is different, they can also mirror one another in a sense. So I genuinely want my story to help other lost migrants see cycles that need to change in their communities, families, and homes. I, additionally, hope the use of television within the delivery of the story helps to connect how many non-native speakers reach survivability and assists in reflecting how many immigrants learn basic communication skills in any country using this particular form of media.

I feel the migrant identity is definitely the primary focus of my writing at this time. I happened to use telenovelas, but the story could have just as easily been called "Spanish *Bachatas* Killed My Mother."

JM: I want to get back to craft talk soon, but let's stick with talk of the themes and culture for a moment longer. Are the whispering iguanas based on real folklore, or is that unique to this story?

DA: Ah, the iguanas! Did you know they are an invasive species on Puerto Rico? I mean, they are everywhere! Iguanas were introduced to the Puerto Rican ecosystem during the 70s, and now you see them on the highways, on riverbeds, in trees, but primarily in farming regions. Considering they have no predators on the island to contend with, they wreak havoc on the agricultural economy.

Now on to why they whisper in the story— when my family and I still lived in Puerto Rico, an iguana came into our home. It was sometime between dusk and dawn and my mother heard my sister giggle as she laid beside her. Being part of a family that believes in *espiritus*, mother assumed my sister was speaking to a spirit and so mother calmly turned to check on my sister. Upon turning, mother realizes my sister is holding and toddler-babbling to a monstrous iguana. Her screams that early morning night were said to have made the walls tremble. It was one of the many anecdotes shared by adults during family parties and gatherings in my youth, always towards the end of the night and always in a circle while they held sleeping cousins. I suppose the personal story above having influenced their inception makes the whispering iguanas unique to SSOKMM, but that is probably not the last time you'll see them in my writing.

JM: I grew up in South Florida, and we have the same exact problem with iguanas. They're everywhere. Their only predators are cars.

I had briefly mentioned it at the top of this interview, but I really wanted to more thoroughly talk about what I called the "purposeful compression" in your story (though it's tangential to our earlier discussion of the structuring). You're compressing so much time here—and many scenes are told in snippets or summary without ever feeling underdeveloped or rushed. Normally, summary is avoided in writing in favor of scene, but I think your summary and scant scenes often work due to the amount of unique specificity and lyricism in your writing. Said another way: this story is able to get away with more *telling* than a story with less lyricism and specificity would be able to get away with. Was this an intentional move? What do you think of the scene-summary dichotomy in writing?

DA: The writing style felt natural. The marriage between the telling of the story and the bringing of the reader into the story-world is pivotal to how the story develops. I enjoy telling a lot to a reader using emotional engagements, which link lyricism and storytelling. Maybe it is because I speak most of my writing before I write it down, but the summary seems to lend itself to helping the reader remain engaged within the tale while shifting with the protagonist. Yet I cannot sit here and boast of some great secret technique that illuminates how and why the compressions and expansions work and maintain each other in a symbiotic way. I thought that breaking the whirlwind of dramatic life occurrences with peaceful poetic self-reflections made up for not telling the in-between. The poetic reflections coupled with the title of each section tell more than the average break and help to place emphasis on the link between place and action so that there is a brace and a dive into each part of the story. Each title guides how the identities within the protagonist see herself and the surroundings, while allowing us to unearth that the relocations taking place are where a new traumatic impression is happening. Sometimes those impressions do not manifest in a plain way because they are ugly to those of us who have experienced them as a result of living in the margins of society. In order to be vulnerable, many writers choose to write about pain in ways that seem beautiful in order to digest those experiences. That is what I tried to do within SSOKMM.

JM: Talk about the tightrope walk between poetry and beauty on one side and sentimentality and flowery on the other. There's so much beautiful language in this piece; talk to me about the difficulties in achieving this rhythm. What are the possible pitfalls, and what difficulties did you have in the writing?

DA: The first line of this story kept dancing in my head for several days before I sat down and put pencil to paper. It just sort of grew from there. Seeing as initially I was under the impression that the first line was leading me towards a poem, when it grew into a story, I knew it had to say something significant while still maintaining a beauty that made it impactful. Thanks to the prompt from class, I also had a specific word count to keep me and my poetic rants in check. In the first stages, it was wordy and possibly dense with over-poetic vagueness in certain areas. For a little, it even got thrown into some less poetic arenas of literary exploration.

It was not until the final revision, before I made my submission, where I noticed the pattern that worked for what I was attempting to do. It's harder than an unripe plantain to write without seeming too full of fluff and flowery sentimentality; however, I am trying to engage in an ongoing dialogue with my writing which leads me to believe that my story must also be able to share something tangible.

So while the work should be beautiful and full of the images of tropical flowers that live rent free in my head, it also has to tell the world of the marginalized immigrant identity and those experiences which also exist rent free in my head. That is how and why I attempt to maintain a balance that keeps a reader interested in the beauty but invested in the tangible experiences being lived within the words of SSOKMM.

JM: Could you talk a little about the revisions process?

DA: So tedious and painful and happy and sad. There are some lines I loved that I had to create better context around. The only person who had edited my work up until that time was me. I had such a weird relationship with editing. In the beginning I felt that, *if my words are so pretty, why would I need to change them?* Then I realized I was not writing for myself and some of my sentences did help in making sense of the textual world. Then you guys came along and stamped some serious editing skills in there. I was intimidated and afraid to receive the first critique from the editors at *Driftwood Press*, but whenever I read your notes, not only were they encouraging, but they were insightful and genuinely helped to guide me through rewriting some of the more whimsical yet disconnected points in the text. Every edit was full of care and thoughtful responses. I am still in awe as to how big of a difference the story has experienced from beginning to end, but it has come together so effortlessly with the help of *Driftwood Press.*

JM: What writers have influenced your writing the most?

DA: The most prolific influence in my life is Mother Earth. To me, she is the greatest composer, poet, artist, lyricist, musician, and writer of all life. I have written the most about nature and have a special relationship with the outdoors and writing.

Textually, writers such as Laura Esquivel, Julia Alvarez, and Toni Morrison have influenced my story telling style the most. They are able to condense large emotional impact into soft beautiful words that deliver these punches full of grit, pain, excitement, and reality, while simultaneously bringing attention to the plight of black and brown livability. Poetically, everything from random poems I have come across in my life, to the works of Kamau Brathewaite and Rita Dove. I am inspired by how they echo the generational effects of colonial oppressions on our minds, bodies, and souls while also bringing in a color and vibrancy of detail that makes it difficult to not imagine specific moments vividly after reading their works. Lastly, it was Eduardo Galeano who made me want to explore my agency via the immigrant identity in occidental culture. His book "The Open Veins of Latin America" galvanized my work towards a literature of substance. It caused me to explore my roots in a literary way, so that I am able to contribute towards an already ongoing dialogue on the marginalization of black and brown folk.

He writes that Latin America and the Caribbean are considered within western culture as "The Nobodies" who

> "...are not, but could be.
> Who don't speak languages, but dialects.
> Who don't have religions, but superstitions.
> Who don't create art, but handicrafts.
> Who don't have culture, but folklore.
> Who are not human beings, but human re sources.
> Who do not have faces, but arms.

Who do not have names, but numbers.
Who do not appear in the history of the world, but in the police
blotter of the local paper..."

In this way, I want to make art that moves others towards their passions, their dreams, and their goals. To take information that is painful and eye-opening and to create agency for our ancestors and the future generations to come has become a purpose I now hold near and dear to my art and soul.

JM: What other mediums have influenced your work? How?

DA: Overall, all forms of art influence my work. Music, architecture, the bell sleeve on the church lady's arm or the stucco churches I've yet to see, all of these and more influence the way I write the world I experience. Even literary essays inspire me and make appearances in my work. Movies and comedy specials also inspire me based on the material, topics, and agency expressed within the work. That is actually how I stumbled upon Galeano's work. Watching John Leguizamo talk about tracing his ancestral immigration and contemporary existence through the work of Galeano and others. So really, anything and everything influences what I write about. Recently, I began a poem called "Walking the Dogs," and it never even mentions dogs. I was inspired by the immense peace I feel when I walk the dogs. I bet someone out there once wrote a poem about Zumba class.

JM: What are you working on next?

DA: A short story that I hope takes over where SSOKMM ends, a lot of poetry, and soon some literary essays of my own. I'm also working on research that has to do with my grandmother Esperanza Isaac and the Latino rights movement during the 80s and 90s. My grandmother had six children and remained married until they became adults (the 80s). After, she divorced my grandfather, then relocated to New York City to pursue a higher education as well as launch a non-profit community health outreach organization called "Casa Esperanza" (House of Hope)—established in the Bronx. I remember spending days there after school during what seemed like such uncertain times in my life. I recently found an article that mentions my grandmother's name and her involvement in establishing this program, which turns out became the primary model for many organizations who do this kind of community outreach. Talk about exciting! Right now, I'm just collecting data, but soon I'll begin to go through it and piece it together and possibly make it into a story or novel.

I have also begun to work on my own research model for the decline of health in marginalized communities and programs that are able to mitigate the necropolitical social structure it seems we are all doomed to perpetuate if we don't get it together. Polar bears are attempting to eat rubber tires and plastic is literally in the rain; antibiotics are becoming irrelevant, and now we will probably be living with the fear of severe "flu like symptoms" for all eternity—so I'm just trying to do my part so it won't be said that I went out without a fight.

JM: That seems a good note to end on. Thanks so much for chatting with me here, Dailihana! Are there any parting words you'd like to leave with our readers?

DA: Thank you for takig the time to speak with me, James. As for the readers, remember to be kind to one another.

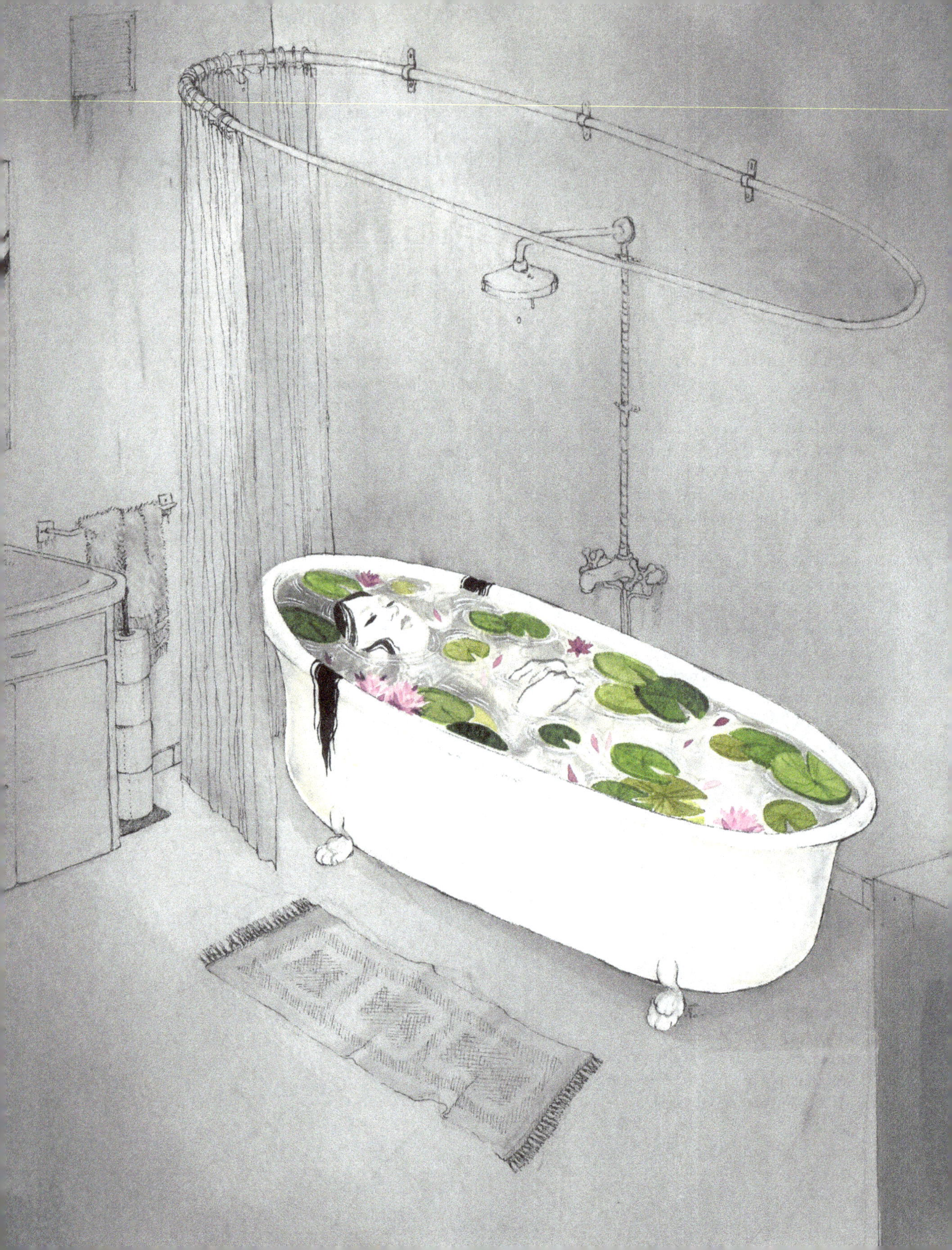

TOO LATE

LAURA OHLMANN

Too late to tell my mother that pieces
of skin were toppling over themselves
on the surface of the water.
Oatmeal suds poured in to cover
the fine bits of hair, the talcum powder
left behind, the disease that would carefully
enter my mother's body and never leave.
The nurse didn't hose
the tub down and douse it
with disinfectant. They didn't
think to cover my eyes
before they lowered her
into the water, the cuts
on her body screaming
in the too-hot sea of skin,
dried flakes staying afloat.
Too late to tell her, *don't go in there.*
I saw something on the surface.
My mother's face was peaceful
hovering above the dense water,
too late to tell her it wouldn't last.

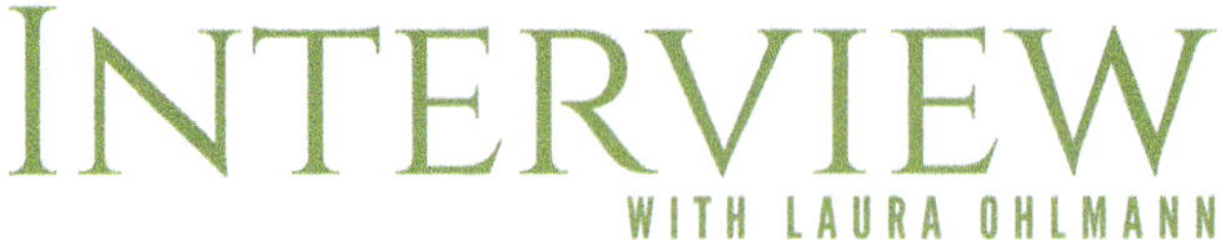

INTERVIEW
WITH LAURA OHLMANN

What inspired the poem?

This poem was inspired by my mother's fight with Sjogren's Syndrome and other autoimmune disorders. Even though it's been over fifteen years since her passing, the loss of your mother never really leaves you. Especially with my mom, I lost her at age twelve, and she was my best companion. Life without her is grimmer and with a little less color, but by bringing her to life in my writing, I'm able to spend a moment of extra time with her.

What was the hardest part about writing it?

The hardest part was reimagining the pain my mother went through. The black skin that formed on her feet and then sloughed off. Then, the skin grafts they took from her thighs to reconstruct her feet and the staples they had to remove from the grafts. It was unimaginable pain for my mother. And all because they didn't disinfect the bath.

How long do you usually spend working on a single poem?

The first draft is typically thirty to sixty minutes. If it's a several page poem, it could be up to two hours. I consider myself a slow writer, and a quick reader. It doesn't benefit my poetry or freelance work, but I enjoy the process.

How long have you been writing poetry? What has changed from your first poem to your newest work?

I've been writing "poetry" since middle school, shortly after my mother passed away. It was a form of catharsis to begin with and leaned on abstractions and emotions to drive it. My poems are more image-driven and narrative now, trying to derive emotion from the reader, instead of pasting my emotions on the page.

Who are some of your favorite poets?

Oh, boy! Don't get me started. My favorites poets include: Sharon Olds, Tracy K. Smith, Phillip Levine, Li-Young Lee, Joe Bolton, Rachel Eliza Griffiths, Rita Dove, Carolyn Forché, and Yusef Komunyakka.

If you had to narrow it down, what three books have had the most impact on your writing?

East of Eden by Steinbeck, *Stags Leap* by Olds, and *The Last Nostalgia* by Bolton. They were some of the first pieces of literature I read as an adult.

What is the best piece of writing advice you've been given?

Don't give up! Focus on imagery, scene, and don't be afraid to be vulnerable. And read, read, read. Read poetry, nonfiction, novels, short stories, graphic narratives, and anything you can get your hands on. Above all, have fun. When you're not, your reader can tell.

Her Name: O.

NIKI TULK

O: the shape an eye makes when dreams are wet and fresh.

O: the shape the mouth carves when the air is suddenly winter.

O: the moon when it is about to give birth to the thin razed version of itself.

O: is the caw of the wound alone in a cave, surrounded by vermin and bones.

O: two mouths keening.

the eye of a fish against glass
the flesh-pink fingernail of an infant
the womb-maw at crowning.

INTERVIEW

WITH NIKI TULK

What inspired the poem?

The poem emerged from a solo performance I did for a women's theatre festival. Creating the show involved journeying inside Ophelia's psyche using video, sound, live cello and spoken poems, live art-making and installation. To create this, I was reading everything I could find on Ophelia, the letter O, cyphers. This led me into various theory-lands—visual art, literary criticism among them, where I came across an essay by David Wilbern that is right at the end of a book called Representing Shakespeare: New Psychoanalytic Essays. The essay is called "Shakespeare's Nothing," and the start of the second paragraph includes the lines: "We can start with the circle: sign of nothing and all, cosmos and zero." I was utterly, instantly captured by this and spent the next few months rearranging words that pulled at me in this chapter, while also adding my own. The concept of O containing the cosmos, and yet a deep ache of absence... This is what feels both magical and devastating about it. I keep rewriting this poem in my head all the time, even though it is technically finished!

What was the hardest part about writing it?

Where to stop. There is no end to O! It is constantly moving in on itself, repeating without doing the same thing, and I literally fell into the O-ness and kept finding creatures nesting within each circle... I still play O games with myself, mostly when I am on long car trips (I have recently moved states) and I didn't run out of Os until I had driven through the entire state of Vermont.

That is the light version. The hard part truly was that each line feels like I am copying something that got burned onto my skin during the writing of the book. What is on my skin is a scar, and a portal, so that the visceral feeling of each line is at times a bit overwhelming. I have synesthesia, so that is probably also part of it, but nevertheless the poem feels unfinished to me, in that it is alive and still has things to say—the cosmic nature of O.

Is this poem categorical of your work? Why or why not?

I would say yes. I strive for each poem to carve out a tiny world, and to do so with as much space in there as possible, and just enough of an anchor for the reader. Each line in this poem has worlds within worlds contained in it, there is a lot of rage and mythic presence in it, a sort of fierce hope and grief together, for me anyway. It feels musical to me, percussive and notated, rather than syntactical, too, which matters as music is huge part of my life too.

Is there anything unique about your personal writing process?

That is hard to know, but I suppose what may be unique is that my poetry comes from being in the world as someone with synesthesia, and as an artist who works in several different media. So when I am creating a work, it gets expressed simultaneously through different projects: writing, movement, improvisation (vocal/sound/narrative/movement), visual and installation art, and sound. So I have all these parallel investigations going on that move inside the same galaxy, but render the concept in different ways. They each dialogue with the other too, so there is this web of co-birthing, or multi-midwifery going on (is that a word?) and eventually one expression of it—one form—will rise to the forefront and demand more attention, and all the other explorations will dovetail into it. They might turn up in the imagery, the musicality, the spatialization of words on the page, the words might have emerged from a physical performance etc.

How long do you usually spend working on a single poem?

Generally the first draft comes fairly quickly, especially if the poem comes after working on the floor in my studio for a while. The re-working of the poem—which can mean stripping it right back to just a few words and re-building it—can take months, sometimes even years. I think it might be more accurate to call myself a re-writer than a writer, actually, as that is what I give the most time to in crafting a poem.

Who are some of your favorite poets?

There are so many! These, though, are the ones I re-read all the time and have to have near me wherever I create anything: Alison Croggon's *Attempts at Being,* Anne Carson—especially *Glass, Irony and God* ... T.S. Eliot, Rainer Maria Rilke, Cecilia Vicuña, Sylvia Plath, Galway Kinnell's *The Book of Nightmares*, the powerful reframing of found text in Heimrad Bäcker's work, NourbeSe Philip's poetry cycle *Zong*! I love June Jordan's and Joy Harjo's work too—too many to list!

If you had to narrow it down, what three books have had the most impact on your writing?

Beloved, Toni Morrison.

I literally would not part from this book after I read it—I carried it against my chest and would not even let anyone else touch it; it was about three months before I could put it down and leave it at home. I had not realized that you could write the subconscious, the truth behind everything, in that way—that you were allowed to. Toni Morrison gave me permission to feel my own suffering, and to let the writing feel it too, although it was years before I was brave enough to do this fully in my own practice. This book seared me in a way no other book has before or since.

Possession, AS Byatt.

She wrote everything for this book—the literary criticism, the actual poetry, interwoven narratives, letters, switching points of view and genres and weaving this enormous love-letter to research and scholarship and the passion in it, all the while critiquing the hell out of it. I was floored by the skill, and she raised the bar for me in allowing research to even be the art.

Glass, Irony and God, by Anne Carson.

The way she gives you these sculptures rather than lines—sharp, charged, they were so good they hurt! "Spring opens like a blade," "the ice has begun to unclench," and "Three silent women at the kitchen table." So much pain carved in those lines, they are visually rich to me, and I feel the temperature and smell them (the joys of synesthesia!).

How would you personally define poetry?

The wrestling match of attempting to take something that can't be languaged and trying nevertheless to language it—and do so in a way that the sound of it, the feel of it thrumming through your body, is not lost because it is disembodied and put on a page. It is different to prose because there is a distilled nature to it, and most of what I perceive in the poem is all the things that are not said and that the space around the words holds instead—the resonance of what's there/not there.

Based on your personal experience, what advice would you give to other writers?

Read across everything you could possibly read, read and listen to as many people as you can, and find a couple of mentors who you believe can see the value in your work and speak to it, while still lifting you up. I would say don't give up, because nobody else can write what speaks through you, whether it gets published or not. Find others who love writing and caring for each other in that practice. And get a rescue dog.

OTHER CYNTHIA

CYNTHIA BARGAR

Rainy day furlough from Glenside
angry you are a mental patient
angry you are compliant
angry you swallow
their Haldol
quiver & twitch.

Your mother
drives to Hunan Pagoda
swerves
on the VFW Parkway.
Water-filled craters.

You ask —   *--shh--*   *--shh--*
Did the other Cynthia
kill herself?

"Yes."
You ask *how.*
"She turned on the gas water heater."

You ask *why.*
"We don't know.
Maybe her boyfriend."

Her boyfriend what?
"Wasn't Jewish." *--shh--*   *--shh--*

You & your mother
round window booth
Hunan Pagoda.
Sip jasmine tea & wait *--shh--*   *--shh--*
for egg flower soup
ma po tofu
egg foo yung.
The rain continues   a big sloppy cascade.

INTERVIEW

WITH CYNTHIA BARGAR

What inspired the poem?

The poem title, "Other Cynthia," is how the speaker has come to think of her father's sister, for whom she was named and who presumably committed suicide at age eighteen. The speaker's mother was pregnant with her when this happened. This poem appears early in my collection, *Sleeping in the Dead Girl's Room*, and begins to braid three of the threads that the poems in the book explore—the other Cynthia's death, the speaker's mental health/unhealth, and the power of family secrets.

What was the hardest part about writing it?

I think the hardest part was that I had the impulse for the poem to say that the speaker had been visited by her dead ancestor, Other Cynthia, the night before she went to a Chinese restaurant with her mother on a "furlough" from the mental hospital. She believes, but is not sure, that the other Cynthia told her that her death had been a suicide. While working on the poem, I struggled with wanting it to be bigger, to say more. I'm glad I was able to exercise restraint.

How long do you usually spend working on a single poem?

I spend as long as it takes—which is a long time. I love writing the first draft; getting going gives me a kind of rush. After workshopping a poem in a writing group, I usually let it sit for a few weeks, sometimes months. If I decide after it's sat a while that I'm going to keep working on it I may or may not show the final version to someone before I send it out to journals.

Who are some of your favorite poets?

The ones I am currently keeping near me are Anne Carson, Don Mee Choi, Lucille Clifton, C.A. Conrad, Kwame Dawes, Jack Gilbert, Linda Gregg, Brenda Hillman, Ilya Kaminsky, Donika Kelly, Phillip Levine, Maggie Nelson, Claudia Rankine, Mary Ruefle, and Danez Smith.

What is the best piece of writing advice you've been given?

Carl Phillips writes and speaks about ways to build or construct a poem with an eye toward "muscularity." I find this very useful—to think about patterns that we "establish and disrupt" within the poem regarding, as Phillips puts it, "syntax, grammar, tense, point of view, sentence length, line length, and sound—which includes rhyme, meter, assonance, and alliteration."

Why Do You Say It's the Life Force? It's a Dying Rose

LAURA ROSENTHAL

The frog lies cracked on the ceramic lawn.
Miles of fingers drip from the willow.

This is not some empty argument
if by *nothing* you mean eyelashes lost in the pandemic.
The dogs sniff, confused, at the old oak's bark.

Think of me as a vat of soup crying out for salt.
If you phoned in the middle of the night I'd think you were a crocus.
You no longer need to wear a mask.

I can't see your face amidst the heliotrope.
The way the bees congregate on its surface—
how to know if it's purple.

A spectacle lens lies on the pavement.
The one-eyed trailer squats on the grass.
The motorcycle's front wheel stares out from its tarp.

Every singed leaf reminds me of home.
Love, the fear in this body knows no borders.

INTERVIEW

WITH LAURA ROSENTHAL

What inspired the poem?

I'd say this poem was fueled by unease about matters both personal and global as well as curiosity about whether a surrealist approach might provide a suitable form for that unease. I wrote the poem while I was participating in a workshop on American Surrealism with the poet Joshua McKinney. One morning, I took a long walk during which I dictated random impressions and thoughts into my phone—oddities such as a glasses lens on the sidewalk, but also riffs on lawn signs, stray associations, and quirky phrases that floated into my head. These impressions became the poem's core.

How much revision went into this poem?

The final poem was the seventh draft within a relatively short period (weeks). I often revise more extensively and over a longer time. However, I had already played with the material quite a bit before the first draft took shape. Each of the images and phrases I generated during my walk ended up as a strip of paper on my kitchen table. After I discarded the lines that didn't grab me, I moved the remaining strips around on the table, Ouija board style, and tried to intuit which lines spoke to one another, which lines felt like they belonged in the same poem. Then I played around with the order. In addition, by the time I generated the first draft, I had already smoothed and refined many of the lines. So I revised considerably, but the revision process took a different form from what I'm used to.

Is this poem categorical of your work? Why or why not?

Stylistically, this poem is different from much of what I've written; it's more overtly surrealist and the associations are looser. However, there are similarities in diction and sensibility; and I feel best about my work, whatever the form or style, if, as here, the phrasing and imagery are visceral and tight.

What is your favorite line from the poem or the line you are most proud of?

My favorite passages in the poem are pairs of lines. I'm particularly fond of the final couplet: "Every singed leaf reminds me of home. / Love, the fear in this body knows no borders." I don't think these two lines would work without the tension created by the strange sequence of images leading up to the last stanza. For that reason, I also love, "This is not some empty argument / if by nothing you mean eyelashes lost in the pandemic." These two lines convey that the context of the poem is contention; I think they clue the reader in to the flavor of the argument, even though the usual information that a reader might use to orient is lacking.

How long have you been writing poetry? What has changed from your first poem to your newest work?

I wrote seriously in college; the impulse gradually attenuated, then fell away almost entirely when I became a lawyer. I returned to the fold, after decades away, about five years ago. When I look back on some of my young adult poems, I admire the intensity, spirit of truth-telling, word play, and access to the stuff of the unconscious. My recent work is more nuanced in its craft, diction, and imagery. The more significant evolution, though, is that now I sometimes have the patience to let the poem find its center of gravity even if it doesn't happen on my schedule, and I understand that revision is a deeper and much more open-ended process than I understood when I was first writing.

PSEUDOCYESIS
~The Symptoms of Pregnancy without a Fetus

BETH SUTER

Schrödinger's baby
in the box of your swelling

inward tug on the navel's root
catfish sucking bait off a hook

bottom feeder in the womb's mud
phantom limbs kicking

your belly's heartless pulse
the negative test like

fighting to reel in an empty line
the pull, sensation of nothing

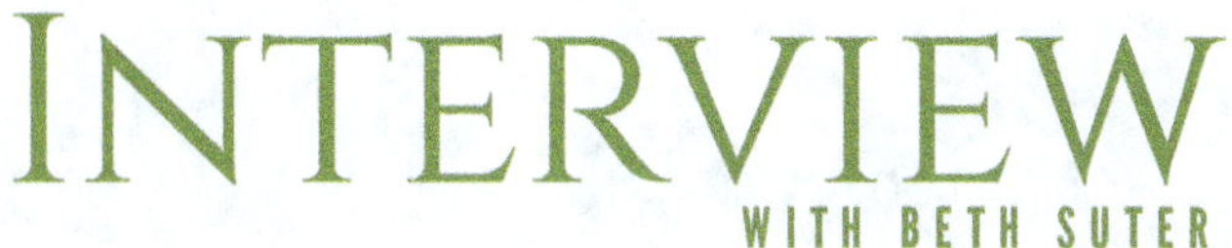

Interview

WITH BETH SUTER

How long have you been writing poetry? What has changed from your first poem to your newest work?

I've been focused on writing poetry seriously for about ten years. Over that time, I've learned to take more risks in terms of subject matter and really embrace the surreal of everyday life.

Who are some of your favorite poets?

Some of my favorite poets are: Joy Harjo, Jane Mead, Lucia Perillo, Jane Hirshfield, Natalie Diaz, and Paisley Rekdal.

If you had to narrow it down, what three books have had the most impact on your writing?

The three books that have had the most impact on my writing are: *House of Poured-Out Waters* by Jane Mead, *How We Became Human* by Joy Harjo, and *When My Brother Was an Aztec* by Natalie Diaz.

How would you personally define poetry?

Personally, I define poetry as a medium for saying the unsayable, an art-form of paradox.

Based on your personal experience, what advice would you give to other writers?

My advice to other writers would be to write what you're afraid of writing. That's your juiciest material.

What is the best piece of writing advice you've been given?

The best piece of writing advice I've been given is: "Don't let the facts get in the way of the truth."

LORD

KARI RUECKERT

lay me down in silence. seeking first
the sanctuary of salt mouths. I am an
ocean apology dripping from the son's
crown. lay me in petal light. in cities.
catching ruptured wings rupturing me
with scripture. I am separation of sound
and its echo. lay me in a seagull. asleep
in marrow. hive surrounded by a hum. I
am a crease of sweat. a lake filled need.
from body to body I am swallowing.
all mercy with feathered lungs. all
body in staccato. Lord lay me in a body
swooned with daybreak. with a field of
monarchs. blessed be the name that's in
my mouth. o holy. this mouth is hunger.
turned inside out. lay me in trespass. in
a violin sound. clutching my spine. I am
all moon circling a strange need. circle
me with clouds of crow. shatter me
in a wing-filled secret. I am a lantern
trapped in a moth dream. lay me Lord in
a taken mouth. O the ache of night. I am
here and I pray for this hidden body to
know me

again and again.

INTERVIEW
WITH KARI RUECKERT

What inspired the poem?

I was thinking about prayer within one out of many traditional frameworks. I started using the ritual repetitiveness of prayer, its established language in certain communities, and molding it into images of intimacy. I see prayer as not just words, but positions of the body.

Is this poem categorical of your work? Why or why not?

The form is not categorical of my work, but the content is. The speaker in many of my poems responds to a specific well-established view of God. Questions I find myself asking are, "What is tradition and what is it within the image and language laid out in a poem?"

The poetic form in "Lord" leans into that.

What is your favorite line from the poem or the line you are most proud of?

My favorite line is, "I am a lantern trapped in a moth dream." I normally look at a certain image from the view of movement. Instead, I wanted to look at the stillness of an object surrounded by movement.

How long do you usually spend working on a single poem?

It depends on the poem, some take a day, while other poems take a year or more. When I'm writing a long poem, it comes in stages where it moves through the body, then I'll write a page or two. The poem will tend to sit in my body again before writing another page. It takes time, trust, and patience.

Who are some of your favorite poets?

K-Ming Chang, Taylor Johnson, Sy Hoahwah, Ilya Kaminsky, and Justin Phillip Reed.

If you had to narrow it down, what three books have had the most impact on your writing?

The Crown Ain't Worth Much by Hanif Abdurraqib. *Registers of Illuminated Villages* by Tarfia Faizullah. *Saudade* by Traci Brimhall.

Based on your personal experience, what advice would you give to other writers?

Trust yourself and the process. Don't allow a culture of constant production define your art.

THERE IS A BLOOMING WRECK IN THE BODY BUT I WISH IT WAS A BLOOMING ONION FROM OUTBACK STEAKHOUSE INSTEAD

DALIAH ANGELIQUE

all this talk of demonology has left me famished,
all this talk of haruspex has left me hollowed

tell me my misery straight from my liver
glean some omen from the sludge of my gallbladder

i won't be satisfied until i'm crowned queen
of the boohoo fembots at Fashion Valley Mall
i won't be satisfied until i'm crowned
Miss Little Caesars Concubine

i am unhinged so my life gets to be a movie, a sexy one
where i weep rubies into the jacuzzi and spill Pepto Bismol
all over my Lazy Oaf coat,
Tragic !

i wear my sadness like a shake and go Party City wig
then i rinse the vengeful goddess out of me with
brine and pool water
Typical !

all this talk of milk has left me, curdled
all this talk of flesh has left me, jagged

tell me i'm sanguine and unassuming
that i can be awful warm and pliable,
cute for a dyke from the right angle

tell me: make a wish for something to happen
and it does

Interview
with Daliah Angelique

What inspired the poem?

I was drawn to the cool-headed hysterics and droll vulnerability flowing throughout the poetry of both Izzy Casey and Chelsey Minnis. The paradoxical duality of their work, at once silly and somber, perverse and glamorous, kitschy and raw, inspired me to wade around and play in the polluted lake of my own psyche. I felt able to express emotions, feelings, and urges through a sardonic funhouse mirror, allowing my Pisces moon to eclipse my Taurus sun. Ultimately, I wanted to write my pain without surrendering to it.

What was the hardest part about writing it?

I feel that writing about mental illness and about the body can sometimes demand a certain responsibility (or, invite moral policing). I think spending a few years in and out of psychiatric institutions has made me wary of expressing myself.

Is there anything unique about your personal writing process?

I think that ninty percent of my writing process is pacing around to music with a Google document open, typing out a few words or sentences until ideas become more fleshed out, and from my pages of notes, a poem becomes more concrete. I'd say that it takes about three to four pages to create one poem.

What is the best piece of writing advice you've been given?

To kill your darlings! This advice was given to me by Kathleen Volk Miller, co-editor of *Painted Bride Quarterly*, during *Frontier Poetry's* Poetry Lab experience. Thinning your poems a bit (perhaps after taking some time away from the pieces after writing to have more of an objective view on your work) can help create more of a throughline for your poems, creating clearer communication between writer and audience.

Who are some of your favorite poets?

Karla Cordero, Izzy Casey, Franny Choi, Richard Siken, Ariana Reines, Chelsey Minnis, Ocean Vuong, Sylvia Plath, and Anne Sexton.

An Aubade

CAROLYN OLIVER

If God breaks your window by reciting an aubade,
tell Her you needed the glass. Start writing an aubade.

Ochre woods at sunrise: a hunter forms his shoulder
around his gun. Through the oaks he's eyeing an aubade.

Like swaying trees, whales dream of sweet dark depths as morning
bleaches blackberry from the sea, sighing an aubade.

Upstairs the bed's gone cold. On a beach we don't deserve
I turn to you and ask, *Are we buying an aubade?*

Who lives to tell of dawn once lovers' bones embellish
broken ground? Somewhere John Donne's replying: an aubade.

Winter: pearl light presses against sleeping snow and skin
warmed where, with tongue or ink, she's inscribing an aubade.

Death paces in the empty tomb, an angel lingers
at the mouth. Whispers sink and rise, fighting an aubade.

Guards slouch round a block; the fallen city waits. Like frost
or smoke two shadows melt away, hiding an aubade.

Clocks blink out, the storm arrives. We never went to bed.
Carolyn, now's no time to be trying an aubade.

INTERVIEW
WITH CAROLYN OLIVER

What inspired the poem?

In a wonderful workshop with Emily Mohn-Slate (with Pittsburgh's Madwomen in the Attic), we read Valencia Robin's "Aubade" from *Ridiculous Light*, and Emily suggested that we try writing our own aubades. I'd written one years ago that I'd never been pleased with and never sent out, so this felt like a second chance. I had ghazals on my mind, and the idea just popped into my head—what if I used "an aubade" as the refrain of a ghazal?

What was the hardest part about writing it?

I think the most difficult part was adjusting the flow of each line, while respecting the limits of the form. I'd write out a couplet, erase all the words except the refrain, and then see if rewriting from memory would give me a smoother line or a new way to phrase an image.

How much revision went into this poem?

This poem came quickly for me—about ten days from the initial idea to the last draft. Most of the revisions were at the line level, since the ghazal's structure is predetermined.

How long do you usually spend working on a single poem?

It varies by poem. Once I get a draft on paper, probably a week at minimum, a month at the outside, if the poem is going to work. That said, an idea might rattle around in my head for two or three years before I start drafting.

Do you work in any other artistic mediums? If so, how do those other genres inform your poetry?

I wish I had an iota of talent as a visual artist, or the ability to compose music, but alas, I do not. I do write fiction, flash and otherwise, and I think that narrative tendency does creep—sometimes stampede—into my poems.

Based on your personal experience, what advice would you give to other writers?

Be persistent. In writing, revising, sending out work.

THE FIRST TIME

SARA MOORE WAGNER

When I lost the baby, the man said   sleep,

          and he was above me holding

her body,   a cloud in the sky,

the slow morphine drip   pat, pat.

Time moves in the hallways and firmament,

and I believe it   when the man tells me

about tissue growth on the outside of my uterus.

I am a house being coated in sugar,   over

and over,   my unlit street stretches out

into a path in the woods,   my baby

walks towards me with her hands   up—

I might push her in the oven to have a taste of what it feels like

to be her, walking so young towards empty.

Give me a way or a pill to make this neater,

give me a knife or a needle: another scene.

Interview

with Sara Moore Wagner

What inspired the poem?

This poem came from wanting to humanize addiction, specifically as it relates to women, and to express how the medical system fails women and often disregards female pain.

How much revision went into this poem?

I worked on the form and ending more than anything. I didn't want to make it "cheesy" or to be overly didactic. I wanted it to be one moment of pain. I had to cut a lot of the places I wanted to explain what I was doing, to say, "this happens to so many women, we suffer, we're disregarded, we want more, so little is offered." I wanted to say that in a measured and quiet way, so it took a lot of working on the breaks and condensing. The ending I cut way back so it could just trail off into the ether, to mimic the subject.

What is your favorite line from the poem or the line you are most proud of?

I am proud of the way I moved from the hospital room to the fairy tale scene, turning the speaker into the *Hansel and Gretel* witch. I hope it shows the false binary nature of how we talk about complicated women who make choices based on desperation and need.

How long have you been writing poetry? What has changed from your first poem to your newest work?

I've been writing poetry seriously for about fifteen to twenty years, if you count undergrad—though I did have a seven year period of not writing or taking care of myself at all. My first poems were very distant, mythic, impersonal. The main way my work has changed is that I let myself in more. I used to be all brain—now I use those other organs. I was also a mess of a person when I started—unmotivated, chaotic. I am still chaotic, but I have more balance now. I care more.

How would you personally define poetry?

This is a tough one! There are a lot of things I say to people who don't like or understand poetry, to get them to see it differently. One is to think of poetry as a cousin of classical music or painting in that it's an attempt to capture a moment or emotion, or to tell a story through tickling the other senses—also that it's not something you always need to "get." You should feel it. We just have language, though, to get someone to feel those great universals. I think every poet might define this based on their own poetry—because there are so many *vastly* different poems. What my poems try to do is to pull the reader into a space using sound and image in a purely linguistic way. I wasn't good at music or painting, so this is how I do it—that's what a poem is. "Every poem breaks a silence that had to be overcome," to quote Adrienne Rich. So many poems speak through giant walls of silence. This is why I started writing poems and why I keep writing them.

Based on your personal experience, what advice would you give to other writers?

You can always be better. This is something I tell myself when I'm in a heavy period of rejection, or when I am feeling too high on the horse. I am not as good as I could be. Read more, revise a lot, write more—you will get better. If I focus on that, I can endure how difficult this world can be sometimes.

What is the best piece of writing advice you've been given?

Let yourself be vulnerable. This is something I have always struggled with, so I will move to disguise myself or hide. Vulnerability speaks more than all the riddles—but I still think a mix of the two is best.

I'M WORST AT WHAT I DO BEST

LAURA BANDY

"Smells Like Teen Spirit" debuts on MTV, September 10, 1991

Ray hands me a beer. He's cheating on me
with my best friend, but I don't know it yet. Ray is my first
love. Mick is Ray's best friend. Mick is in love with me
but I don't know it yet. The Coors can is warm

and I think how beer doesn't taste very good. That will change
but I don't know it yet. Ray's mother in bed upstairs with satin sleeping mask
and "Sounds of the Beach" on repeat. I will date Ray for two years and never
meet her, but I don't know it yet. Ray is wearing a child's Hawaiian shirt

that half covers his frame. He is the first of three men over 6'5" that I'll date, all just
taller than my father, but I don't know it yet. His father left money on the table
for pizza before leaving. He's got a tumor in his gut like a sailor's knot
but we don't know it yet. Ray loves boats. When his father dies

in six months, Ray will row his father's boat out to the middle of Lime Lake
and sink it, almost sink himself, but we don't know it yet. Mick thinks
we should spend the money on nitrous. He buys oversized balloons to speak
in squeaks before really sucking it in. After inhaling eight balloons, I will stop breathing

for a minute, but we don't know it yet. Roy says the balloons make it a party
and we need noise, so he turns on the TV. Next week watching *Barney Miller*
and cleaning his gun, he will fall asleep and his brother will load it. Ray will wake, not like
the episode, and shoot Wojciehowicz, but we don't know it yet. I want to watch *120 Minutes*

and the boys bump into each other reaching for the remote. I will sleep
with both of them before morning, but we don't know it yet. A music video
on screen from a band we've never seen and Ray turns it up. The singer mumbles,
screams, and we're transfixed. Mick asks, *what's he saying?* but no one knows it yet.

INTERVIEW

WITH LAURA BANDY

What inspired the poem?

I love this question. I remember sitting in the University of Southern Mississippi library (I am always most at peace in libraries) and thinking, "Hmmm... I really need to get something down for workshop." It was quiet in the library, of course, and I was enjoying a kind of low-level meditative state as two students passed by holding hands; he staring at her with devotion it seemed to me, and she looking away at—what? I'm not sure, but she slipped her hand from his grip and trotted away without a backwards glance. "Well, they're doomed," I thought, "but he might not know it yet." That line began a kind of music in my brain, encouraged by the exterior hush of my surroundings, and I had a flash of one of my own doomed relationships from youth. The poem itself is a mix of fiction and reality, but what I really remember about the poem process was how important the rhythm, the cadence felt as I was writing. There is no formal meter or structure (other than the repeating line) imposed on the poem, but I could feel an insistent beat as I was writing, which was new and welcome to me in my writing process. I've been much more aware of cadence and sonic pleasure in my poetry since that time.

I wonder what happened to the couple in the library? I wish I knew.

What came easiest when writing this poem?

The association of images was dreamlike for me. I allowed my subconscious self to take the lead as I moved from line to line, and the connections were loose, strange, nearly mystical—they were not linear and seemed to come from some other place or other self. Giving over felt amazing.

What is your favorite line from the poem or the line you are most proud of?

The line I've always enjoyed from the piece: "His father left money on the table/for pizza before leaving. He's got a tumor in his gut like a sailor's knot/but we don't know it yet."

For me, this is the turning point in the poem—the locus, the shift, the moment when the stakes are raised. The turn is always exciting in the writing process, especially when it arrives unbidden, as these lines arrived for me on the page.

How long have you been writing poetry? What has changed from your first poem to your newest work?

I've been writing poetry with some seriousness since I was an undergraduate, so that has been...some years now... (20+ years!). My early poems were elliptical, puzzling, hermetically sealed—I did not understand the importance of clarity or the image. The privilege of great teachers like Michael Van Walleghen, Brigit Kelly, Angela Ball, and Michael Robbins, along with reading poetry widely opened up possibilities, and my poetry changed radically. I strive now for precision in words and image, for clarity of the clear stream rushing over the polished rocks below, and for linguistic play and surprise in the lines. I think I will always be a Midwestern poet—I can't seem to stop writing about cornfields.

What is the best piece of writing advice you've been given?

From the poet, Michael Van Walleghen, my teacher and great inspiration—"The surrounding nonsense can get loud, but don't let it drown out the poetry. The poetry—the poems themselves, the writing of—the poetry is always good."

This is Not About the Birds

HEATHER BARTLETT

the crows have come
back   so many
black wings
among the branches
that I can't remember
when the leaves fell
away   before
you said
no   I said
this is not about
the way things drop

this is not about
the birds   you said
the word for this
kind of flight is
invitation   to the crows

a woman's open hand looks
like a question
to the crows   her body
is thicker
than its shadow   the word
is *invasion*   no

this is not
a metaphor   a woman opens
her hand
to block   her body
weeps   now
they all want
a turn at the flesh   no
the crows
are not perched
in waiting   you know
the word for this

INTERVIEW
WITH HEATHER BARTLETT

What inspired the poem?

Whenever I look out my office window, I see the tops of tall trees that line the parking lot. In the winter time, at dusk, the bare trees are full of crows, so many that it looks like the leaves have suddenly reappeared in the branches. The birds are loud and formidable, and every time I walk to my car, I know they could drop down on me at any moment. They're terrifying and amazing.

What is your favorite line from the poem or the line you are most proud of?

"this is not about / the birds"

This line, which also became the title, was a turning point for me when writing the poem. I had been carrying around the image of the crows in the trees for so long. It consumed me for quite a while, but I didn't really know why. It wasn't until I found this line that the poem actually started to take shape.

Is there anything unique about your personal writing process?

I'd love to say something like, I get up at 5AM every day to write, or I sit down at the desk and write until the poem is done. But I've never been that kind of writer. Sometimes I can get lost in the writing process. I will sit down to write for a few minutes, and suddenly the whole day has passed and my stomach is growling. Sometimes I will sit down to write and get right back up again to mop the kitchen floor or reorganize a cabinet. And sometimes I can't even sit down to write in the first place. It depends on the poem. It depends on the day. When I wrote this poem, I also reorganized an entire closet.

How long do you usually spend working on a single poem?

I'm always working on poems. They're never done.

Who are some of your favorite poets?

I will always reach for June Jordan, Audre Lorde, Adrienne Rich, Ellen Bass, Sharon Olds, Li-Young Lee, Mary Ruefle, Marie Howe, Donna Masini, Jan Heller Levi. Currently, I'm carrying around work by Chen Chen, Jericho Brown, Maggie Smith, and Donika Kelly.

If you had to narrow it down, what three books have had the most impact on your writing?

Mules of Love by Ellen Bass.

The Good Thief by Marie Howe.

Direct by Desire: the Collected Poems of June Jordan (this is probably cheating).

FLIGHT RISK

CHRISTINE BYRNE

Credits for the birthday cake and the porcelain
Fancy sandwiches

Weren't perfect

I taught you
Tired trees sapped over
My mistakes are taken & I've warped you

I get you're angry, still
Messy, I'll take this seriously

Don't you wonder about destitution
The way fire lights
Everything that's happened to me

I've lived years past what you've imagined
My face used to look like
There were men and abbreviations

Don't you think I've gripped
Pieces too, that I've wretched and hunched and
Cut my bled color

Don't you wonder about the rain
My conclusion of God
The reason I named you after

How to run from everything
Good, heaven, the prices of meat from the deli market specified
In brand order
Encased in glass
Sitting in chilled slabs

PEASANT DISHES

CHRISTINE BRYNE

In the waiting there is an aggression of sticky notes. *Today is a good day to...*

Within the guidelines of summer: losing against the postal service, brushing along women's clearance racks, my mother's passivity. And the letters:

Angela,
It's marigold season. It reminds me of that day we were gardening and you accidentally touched the dead bluebird. Or

Dear Angela,
You are handed to me in dishes from neighborhood's condolences—so many casseroles

And then the rushing—forward walls of silly boxes, movement blowing our hair across our faces in the most important moments—become ordinary.
Everything else unalive: gesture, a little spill, nervous brushing.

As if *then* and *suddenly* don't exist within the same impulse, as if it wasn't the same as those seconds you snuck greedily
As if *then* and *suddenly* don't amount to that fact that those words can only allude to your space, which we periodically try to clean over,
which happened in such an instance you find yourself saying words that all mean the same thing: *no, impulse, Angela.*

Dear Angela,
I had another moment. Believing you were somehow leaning the world, whispering to me in your teasing little voice when telling stories, "*And then suddenly—*"

Then suddenly August, the man who came to live in the empty bedroom, standing on his toes to kiss my mother, who confined herself, moving every way of white robe. How he brought an enormous cooking pot and spent the afternoons slicing onions, concoctions of broth, noticing my nervous "And who might you be?"

All adolescent standing, "Do you want a taste?"

How mother never noticed him asking, braided rolls in her anxious hands, the flour fracturing the air like tangible stillness, pushing with the rise of dough.

Maybe it's all distorted now, these waiting faces: Our gestational summers, heatless, which existed in our thirteen-year-old skinny legs propelling us, planning us—
Dawdling at the counter with the quarters in your pocket.

The man sucking on your littlest finger through the car window.

Your specific looks, always so impatient, as if expecting the grand volume of life to occur at every moment, countered by waiting, repeating, growing too slowly, saying with your eyes Angela, Dear

Boxes of letters I wrote you as the man began sleeping in your bedroom, mother's craning over the table, breaking fingernails one by one under the weight of its legs: Dear

Angela, Dear Angela,

The kitchen. Another dim single light bulb. Stirring endlessly. Angie. Cupping in water to thin the broth. The way his hair grew longer into winter and I once saw a lonely particle of him floating in the yellow and onion and sink, in the smallest servings of soup
ladled, and then no more.

BEEKEEP

CHRISTINE BRYNE

She runs my life in front of me like a faucet
(false conceptions) (mis-directions)
I was engaged to the beekeeper

It's any other November dinner. Dad
Won't emerge from the shed. She's drinking something yellowy
Is too nervous to ask me

*Beekeep: to be kept

(he'd lay his glasses on my bare stomach sleeping) (only used
his left hand)

Do you remember, when you were younger, scared of lightening?

Thunder is actually—sound of air—do I have that? —The sound of air moving
the—expansion of the path of lightning—the process of surrounding—of downing,
—the sound of invisibility moving

What's he like? This fiancé...
Lives by the apiary, works with honey—

—all that moving—upward—as a child he got his hand stuck
in the electronic garage door opening—all that
upward moving—

Mother, stop this talk about the weather.

I think about eating out of his refrigerator forever
The different whatevers of sentiment.

Who told you about my engagement?

She swallows oblivion with her afternoon tea,
& I—was in the meantime—thinking about carrying

On—what I mean to say is that I wish
    We were table condiments, to be shook out of our whole lives

He kept saying "allogamy" like "love me"

Pocketing & unpocketing
        his mangled hand his
Simple, inaudible
    Cautious touching

I was still a waiting room   *the sound of invisibility moving*
Checking myself

    In all mimicking surface. I liked
That he never

Reminded me of anywhere

JIM STILL-PEPPER'S
BREATH IN LUNGS

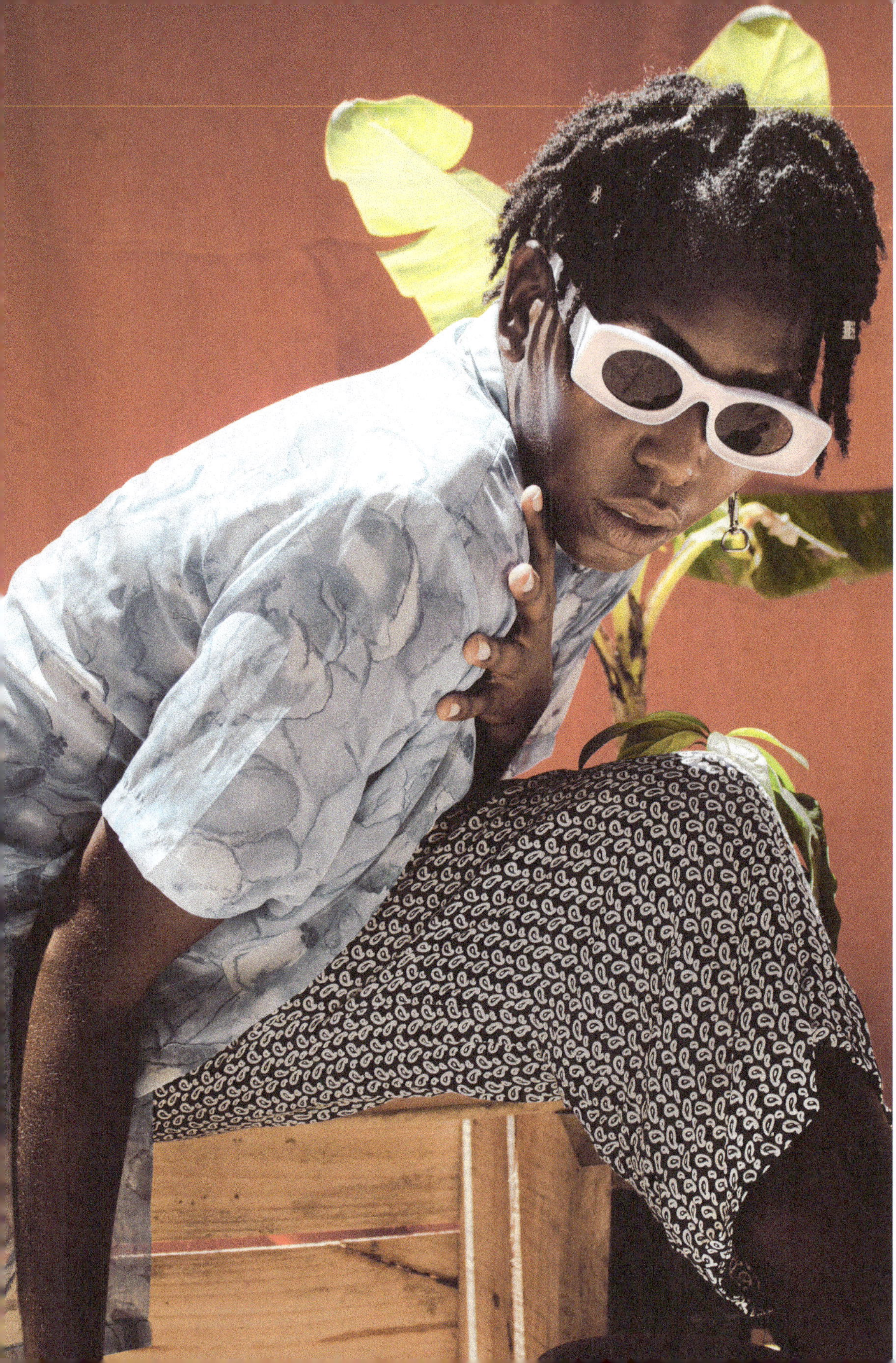

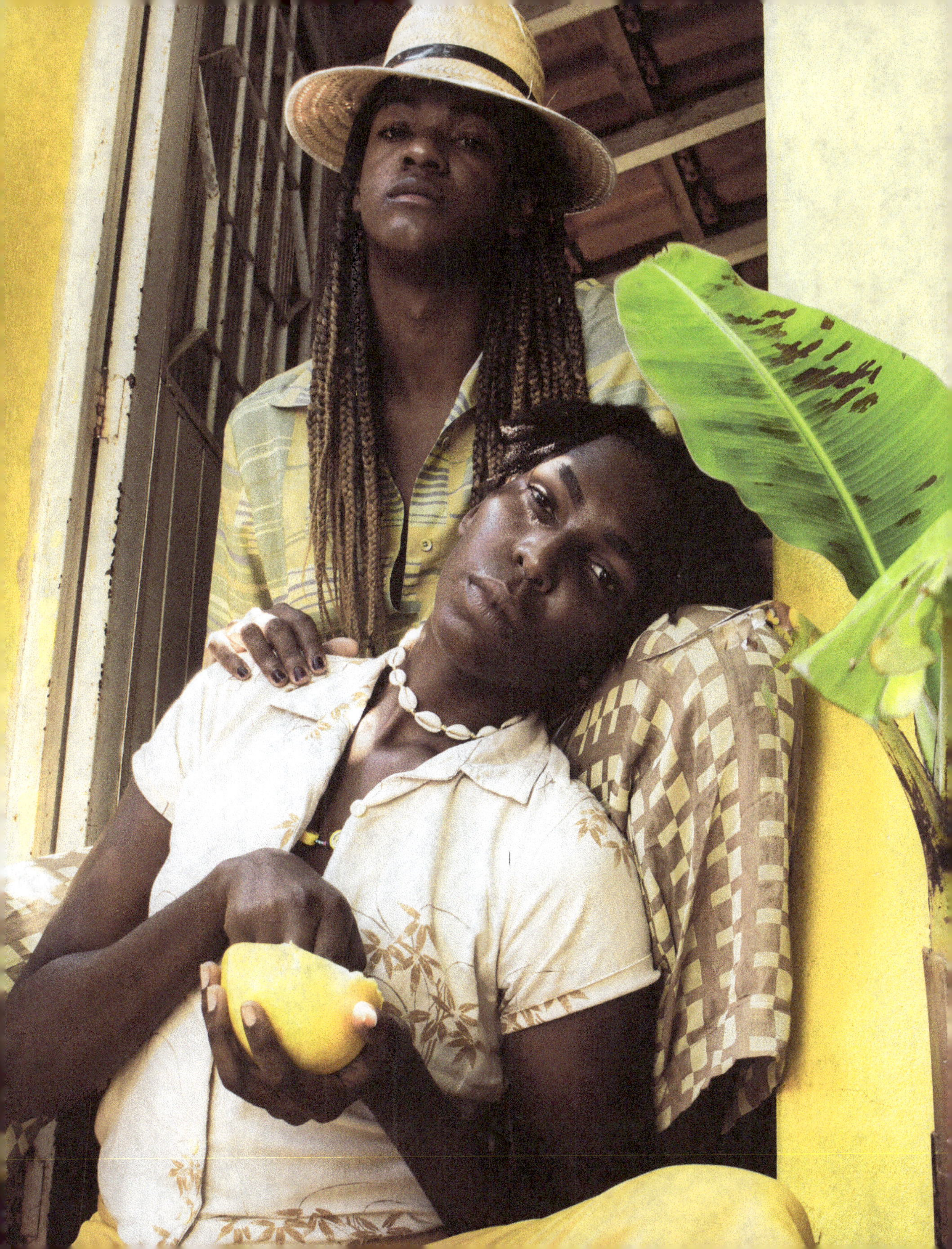

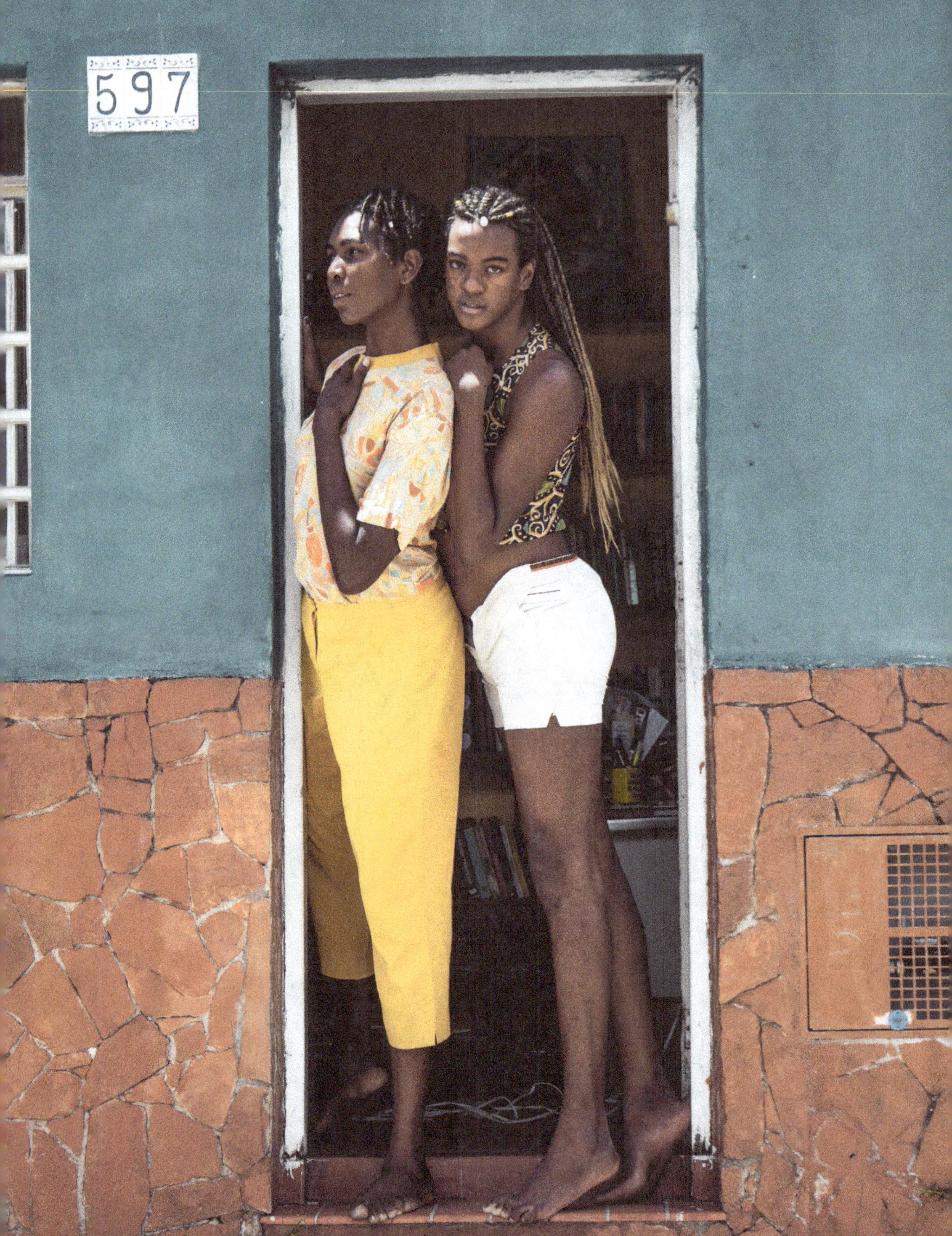
597

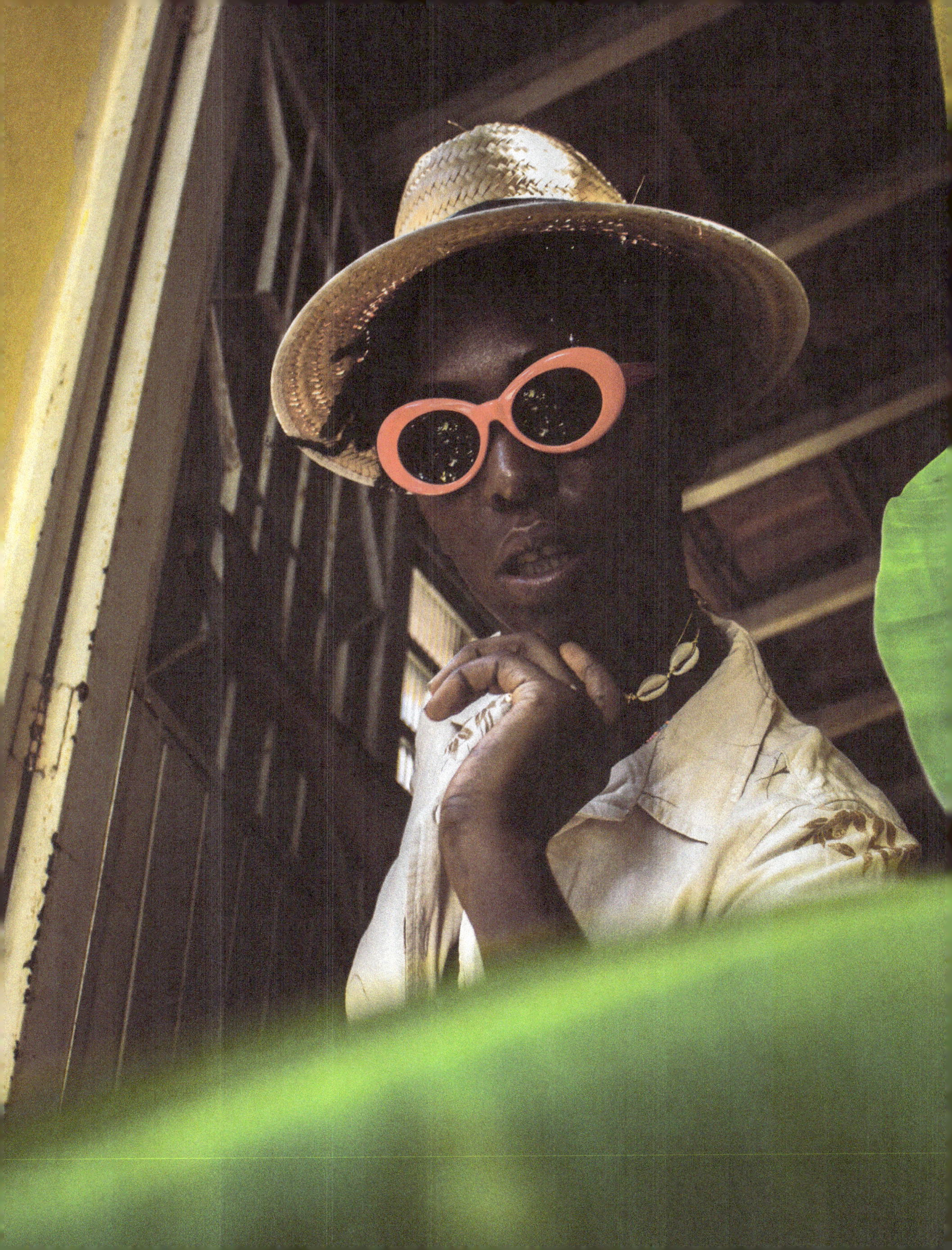

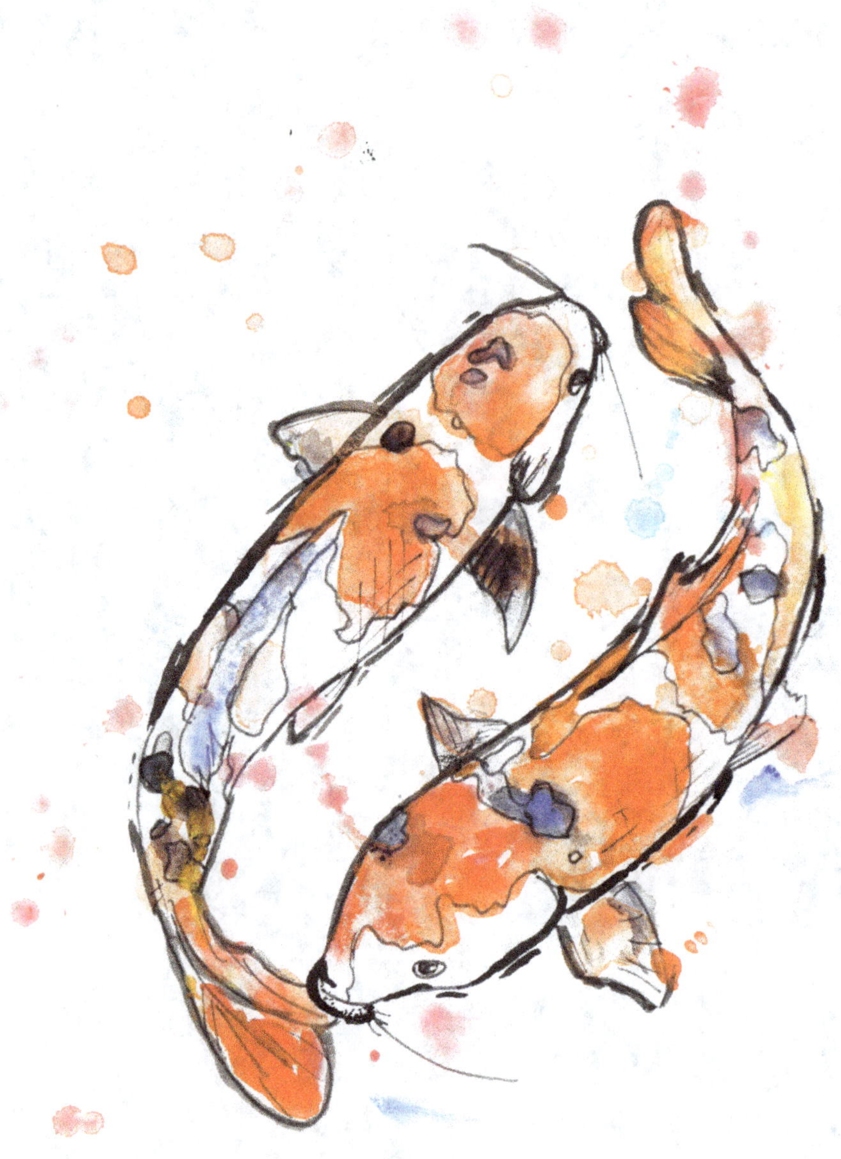

KELSEY M. EVAN'S
KOI

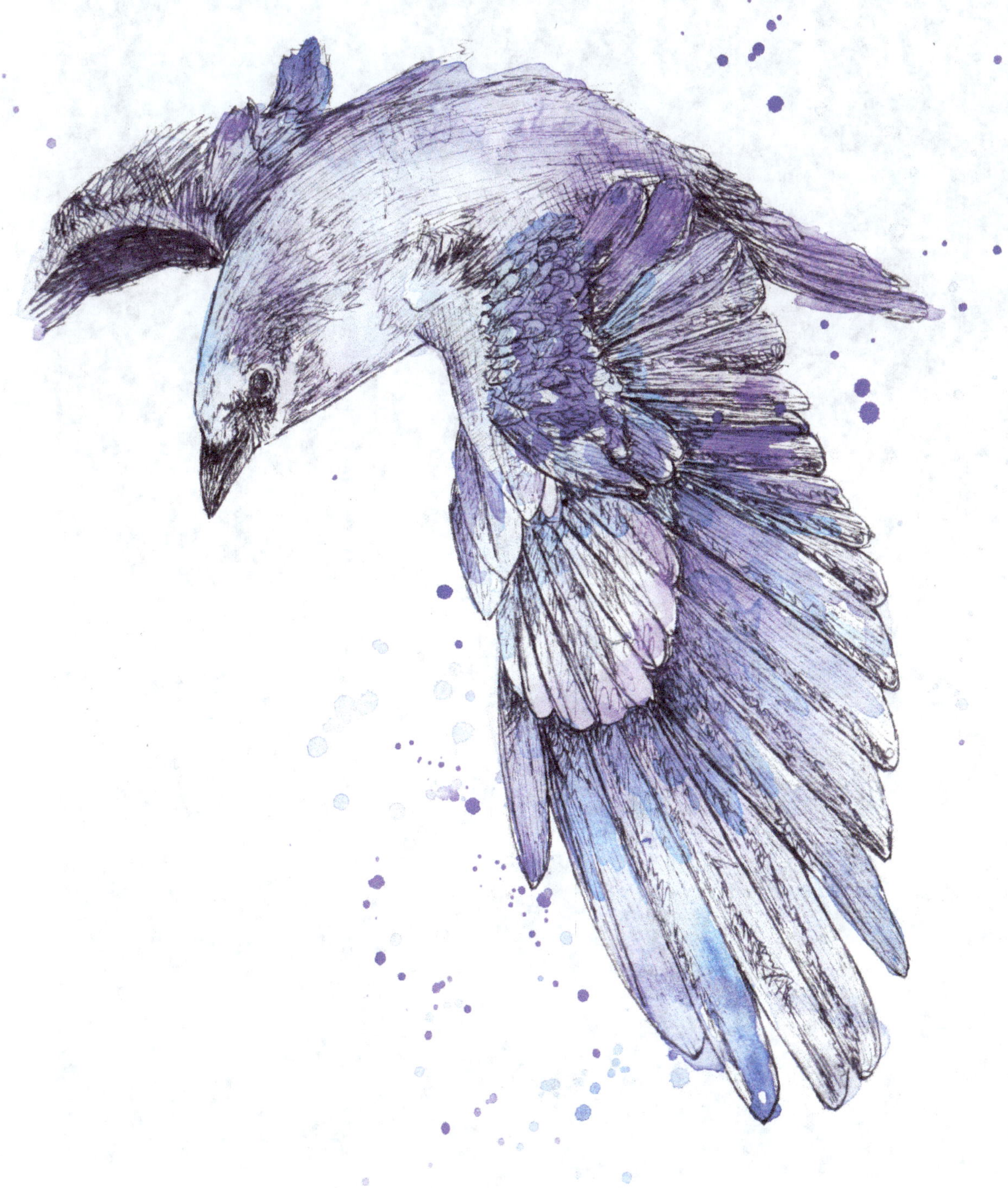

KELSEY M. EVAN'S
BIRD

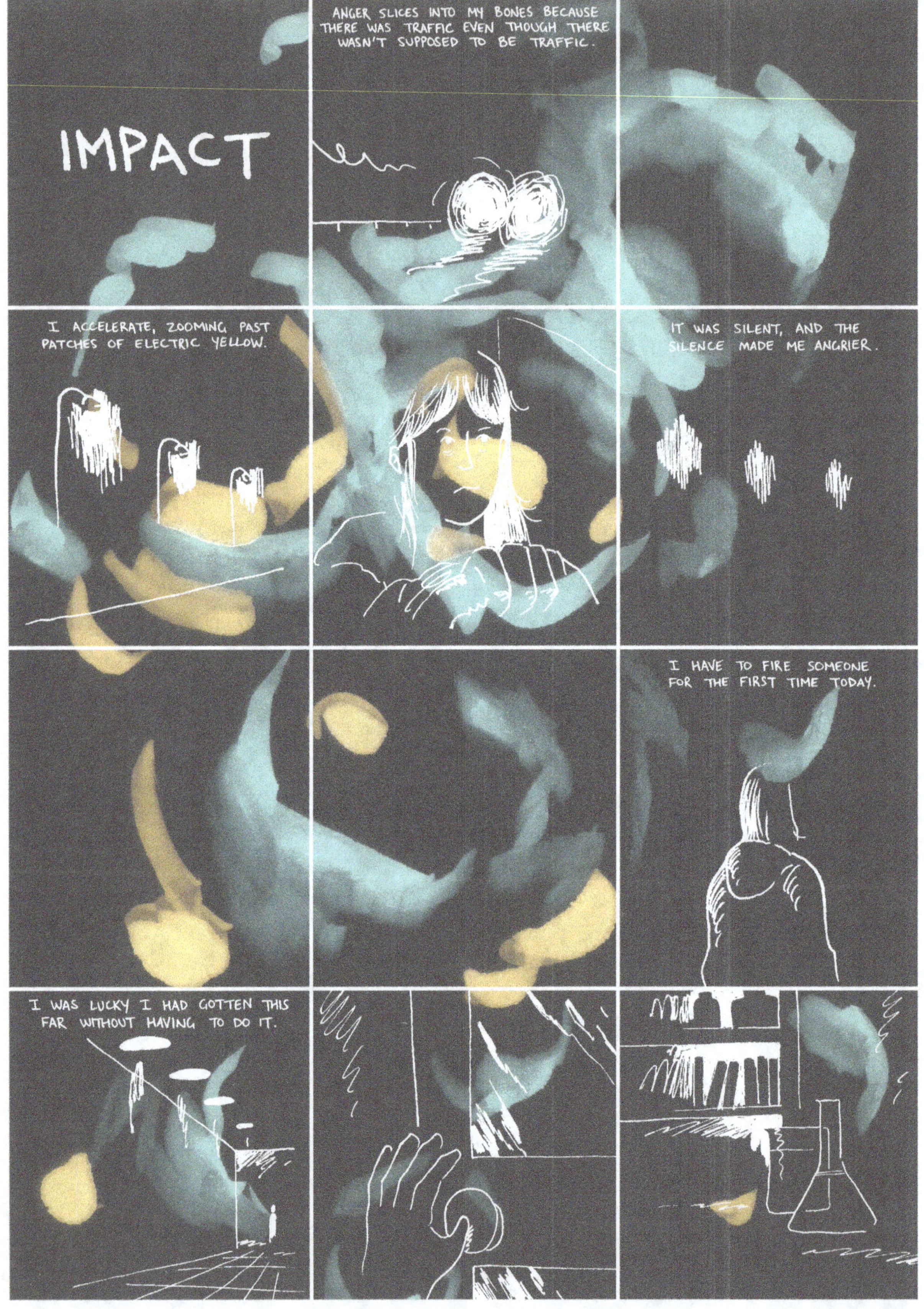
IMPACT
ANGER SLICES INTO MY BONES BECAUSE THERE WAS TRAFFIC EVEN THOUGH THERE WASN'T SUPPOSED TO BE TRAFFIC.
I ACCELERATE, ZOOMING PAST PATCHES OF ELECTRIC YELLOW.
IT WAS SILENT, AND THE SILENCE MADE ME ANGRIER.
I HAVE TO FIRE SOMEONE FOR THE FIRST TIME TODAY.
I WAS LUCKY I HAD GOTTEN THIS FAR WITHOUT HAVING TO DO IT.

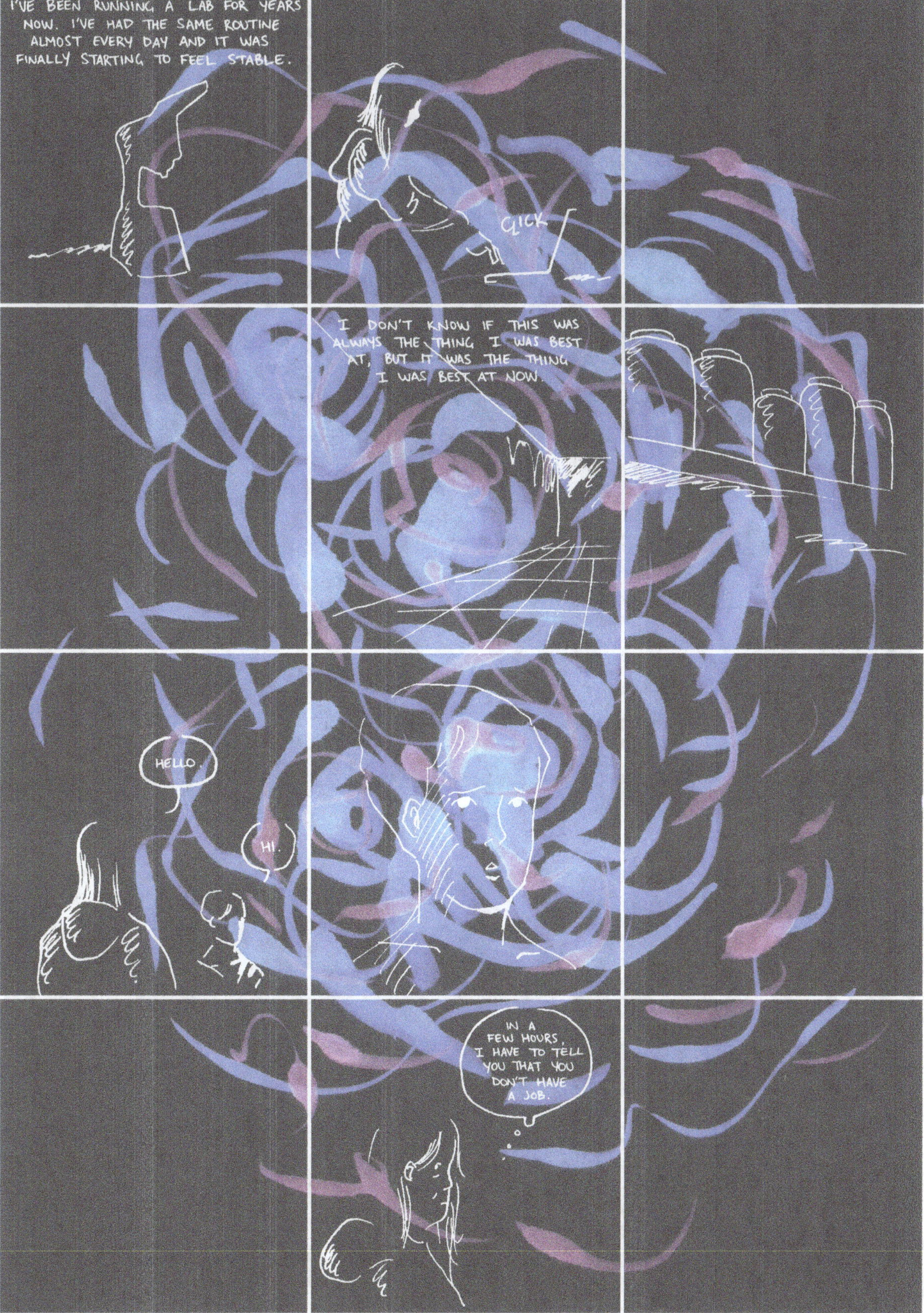
I'VE BEEN RUNNING A LAB FOR YEARS NOW. I'VE HAD THE SAME ROUTINE ALMOST EVERY DAY AND IT WAS FINALLY STARTING TO FEEL STABLE.
CLICK
I DON'T KNOW IF THIS WAS ALWAYS THE THING I WAS BEST AT, BUT IT WAS THE THING I WAS BEST AT NOW.
HELLO.
HI.
IN A FEW HOURS, I HAVE TO TELL YOU THAT YOU DON'T HAVE A JOB.

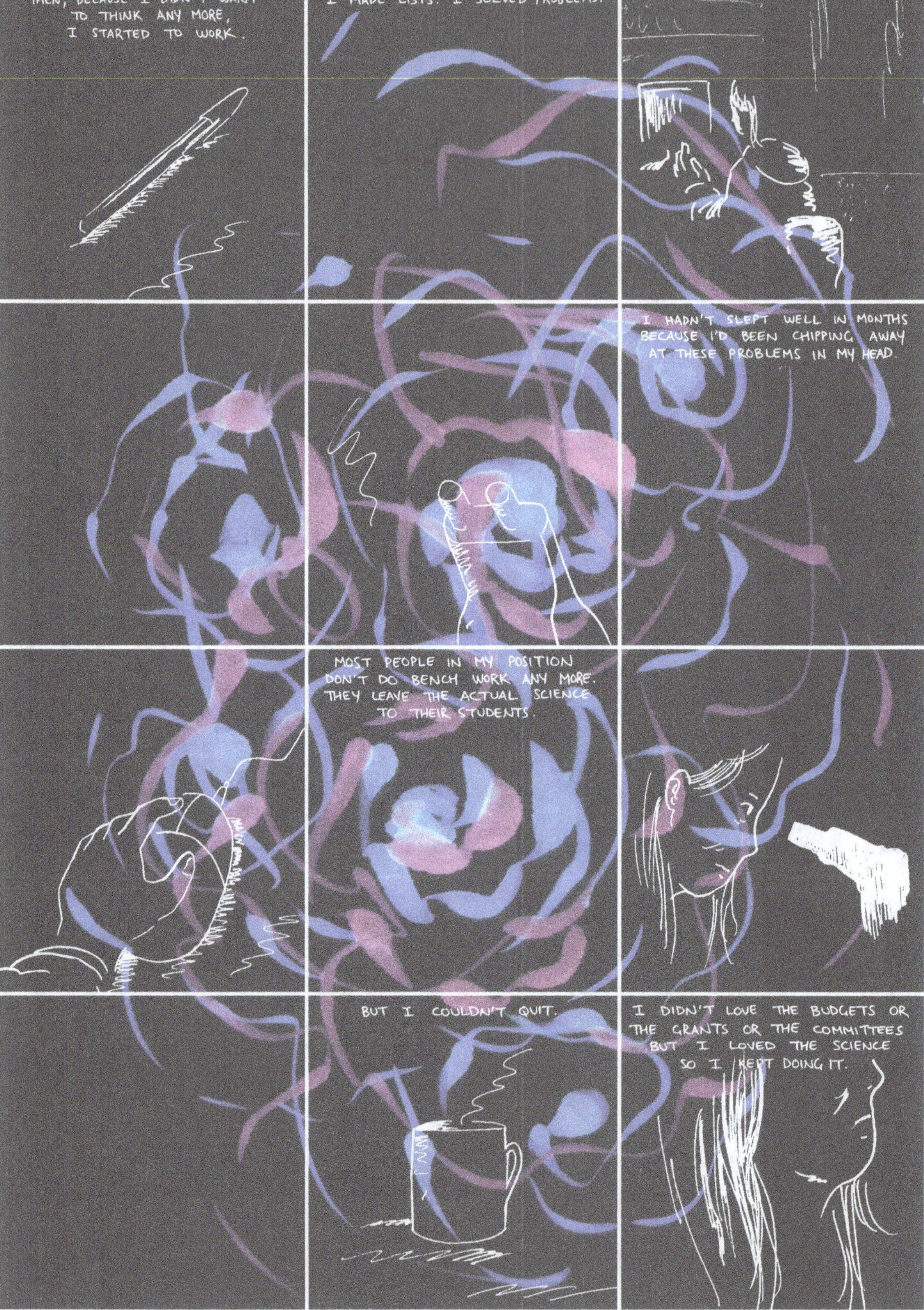
THEN, BECAUSE I DIDN'T WANT TO THINK ANY MORE, I STARTED TO WORK.
I MADE LISTS. I SOLVED PROBLEMS.
I HADN'T SLEPT WELL IN MONTHS BECAUSE I'D BEEN CHIPPING AWAY AT THESE PROBLEMS IN MY HEAD.
MOST PEOPLE IN MY POSITION DON'T DO BENCH WORK ANY MORE. THEY LEAVE THE ACTUAL SCIENCE TO THEIR STUDENTS.
BUT I COULDN'T QUIT.
I DIDN'T LOVE THE BUDGETS OR THE GRANTS OR THE COMMITTEES BUT I LOVED THE SCIENCE SO I KEPT DOING IT.

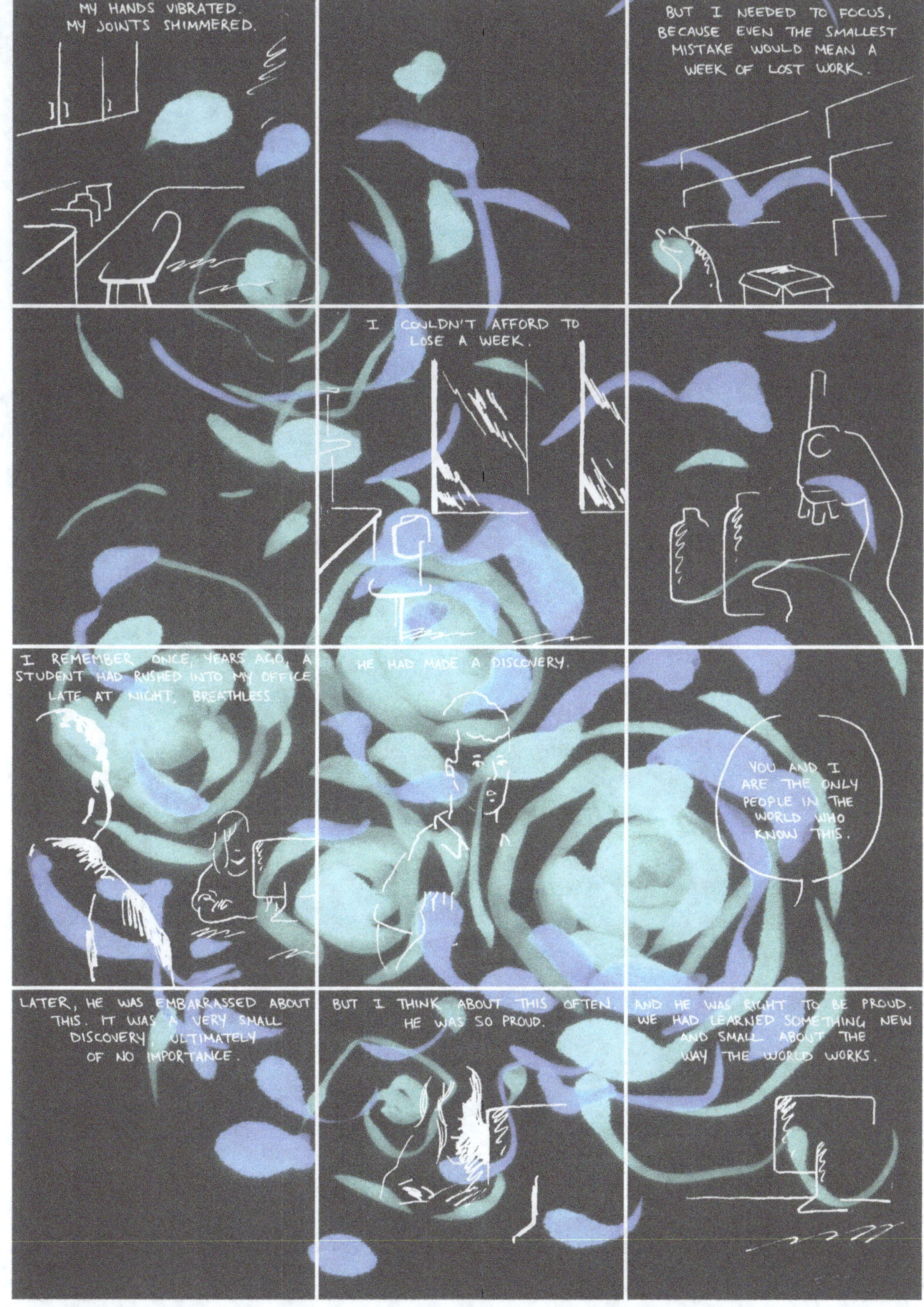
MY HANDS VIBRATED.
MY JOINTS SHIMMERED.
BUT I NEEDED TO FOCUS, BECAUSE EVEN THE SMALLEST MISTAKE WOULD MEAN A WEEK OF LOST WORK.
I COULDN'T AFFORD TO LOSE A WEEK.
I REMEMBER ONCE, YEARS AGO, A STUDENT HAD RUSHED INTO MY OFFICE LATE AT NIGHT, BREATHLESS.
HE HAD MADE A DISCOVERY.
YOU AND I ARE THE ONLY PEOPLE IN THE WORLD WHO KNOW THIS.
LATER, HE WAS EMBARRASSED ABOUT THIS. IT WAS A VERY SMALL DISCOVERY, ULTIMATELY OF NO IMPORTANCE.
BUT I THINK ABOUT THIS OFTEN. HE WAS SO PROUD.
AND HE WAS RIGHT TO BE PROUD. WE HAD LEARNED SOMETHING NEW AND SMALL ABOUT THE WAY THE WORLD WORKS.

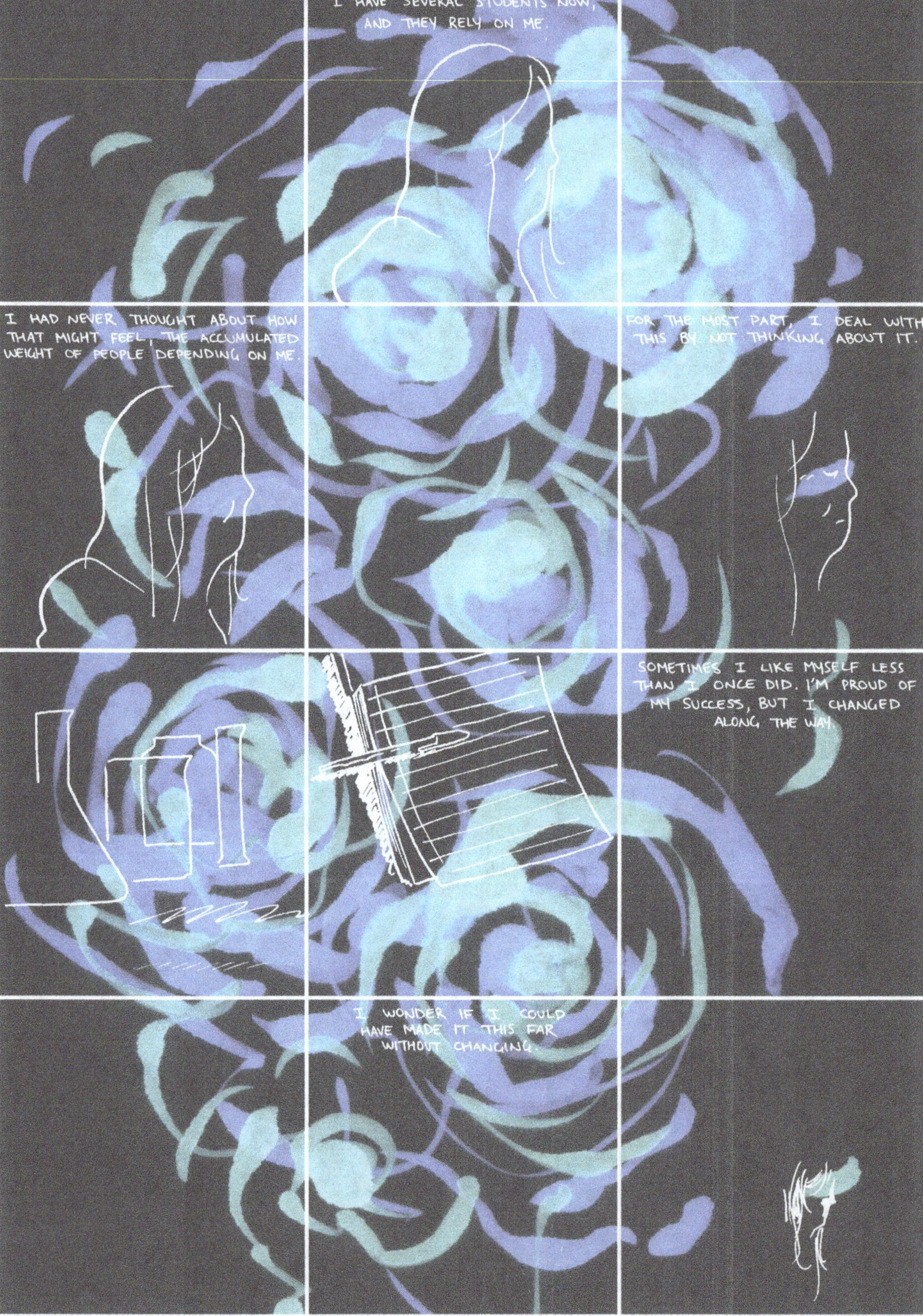
I HAVE SEVERAL STUDENTS NOW, AND THEY RELY ON ME.
I HAD NEVER THOUGHT ABOUT HOW THAT MIGHT FEEL, THE ACCUMULATED WEIGHT OF PEOPLE DEPENDING ON ME.
FOR THE MOST PART, I DEAL WITH THIS BY NOT THINKING ABOUT IT.
SOMETIMES I LIKE MYSELF LESS THAN I ONCE DID. I'M PROUD OF MY SUCCESS, BUT I CHANGED ALONG THE WAY.
I WONDER IF I COULD HAVE MADE IT THIS FAR WITHOUT CHANGING.

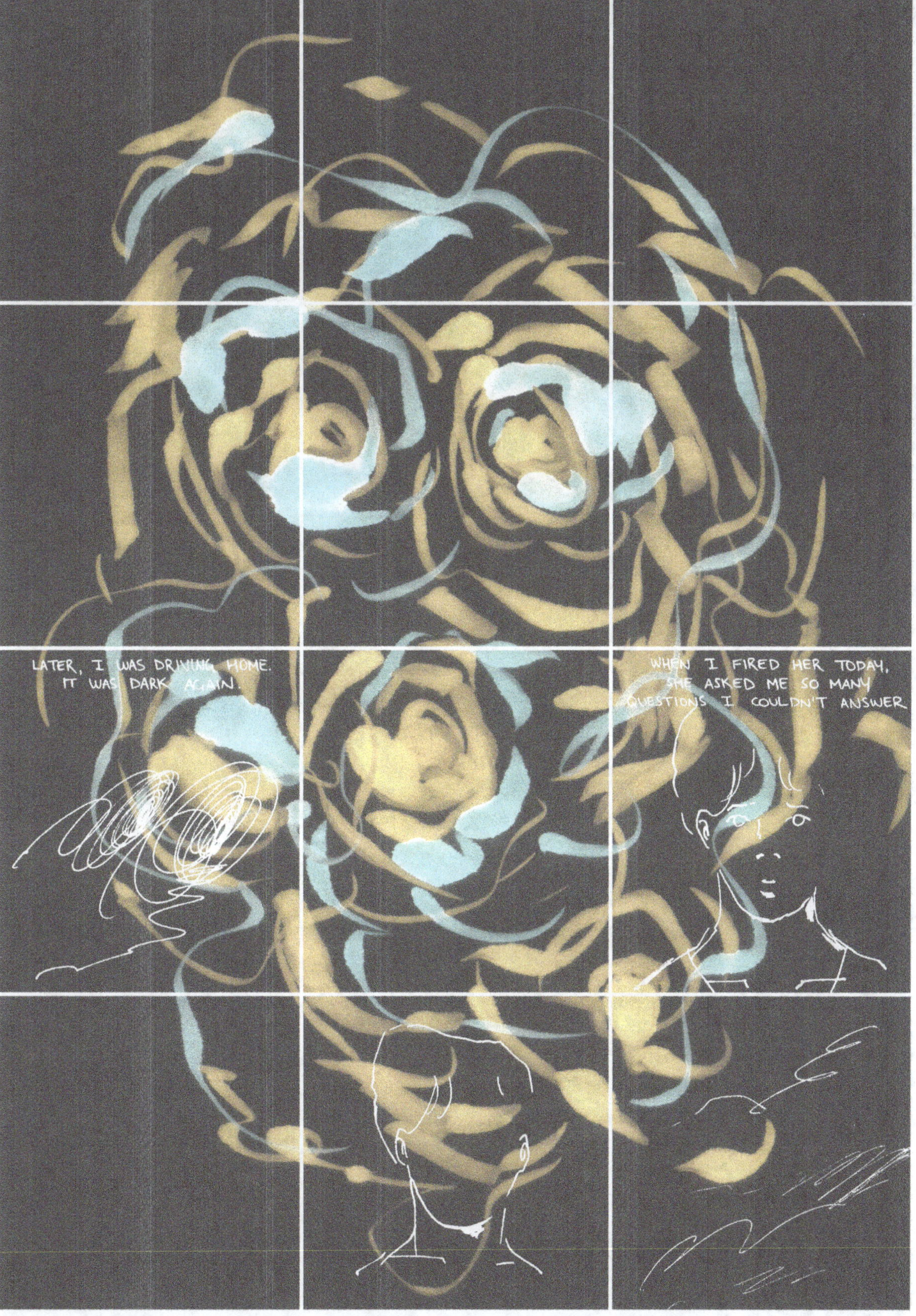
LATER, I WAS DRIVING HOME.
IT WAS DARK AGAIN.
WHEN I FIRED HER TODAY,
SHE ASKED ME SO MANY
QUESTIONS I COULDN'T ANSWER

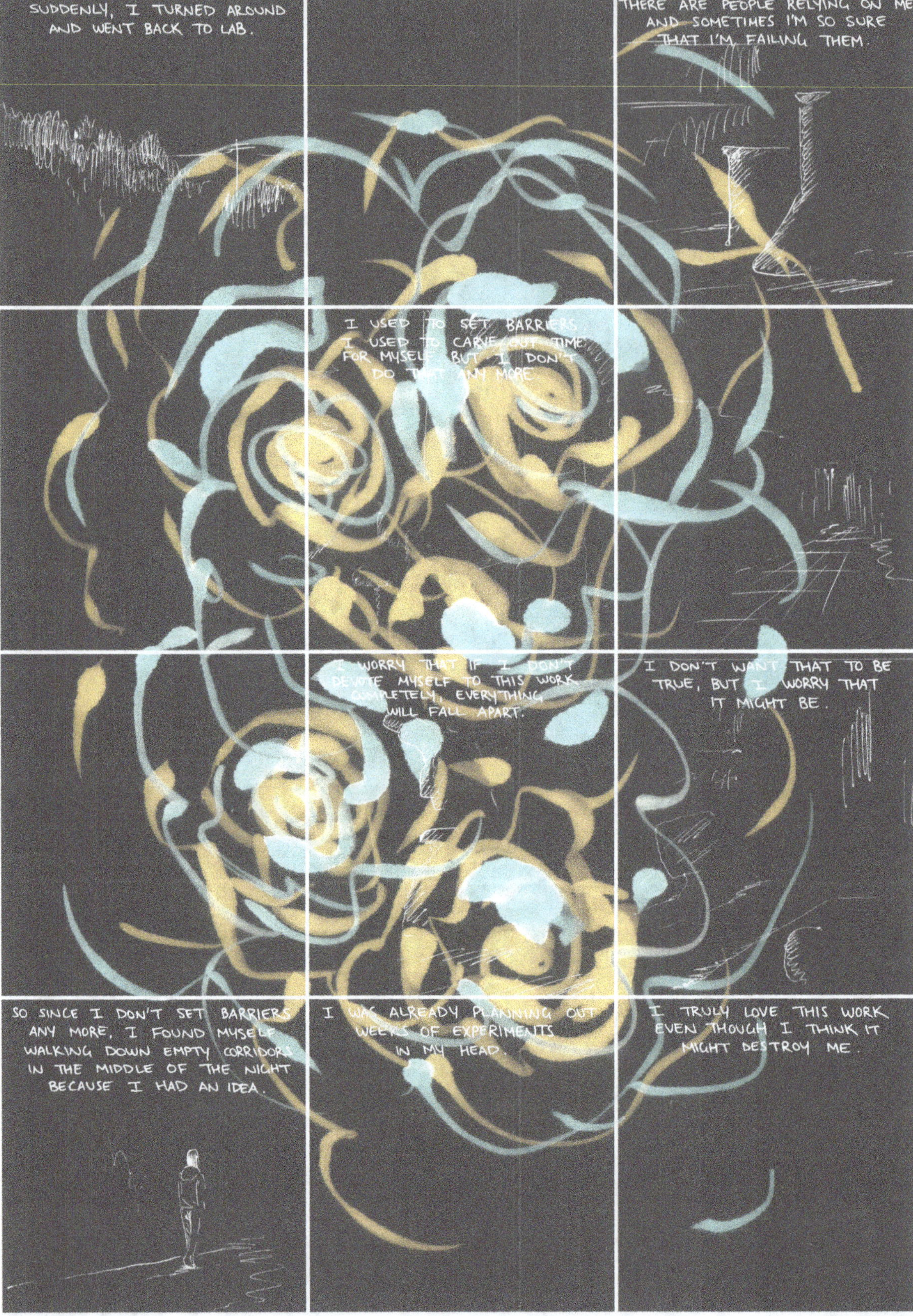
SUDDENLY, I TURNED AROUND AND WENT BACK TO LAB.
THERE ARE PEOPLE RELYING ON ME AND SOMETIMES I'M SO SURE THAT I'M FAILING THEM.
I USED TO SET BARRIERS. I USED TO CARVE OUT TIME FOR MYSELF. BUT I DON'T DO THAT ANY MORE.
I WORRY THAT IF I DON'T DEVOTE MYSELF TO THIS WORK COMPLETELY, EVERYTHING WILL FALL APART.
I DON'T WANT THAT TO BE TRUE, BUT I WORRY THAT IT MIGHT BE.
SO SINCE I DON'T SET BARRIERS ANY MORE, I FOUND MYSELF WALKING DOWN EMPTY CORRIDORS IN THE MIDDLE OF THE NIGHT BECAUSE I HAD AN IDEA.
I WAS ALREADY PLANNING OUT WEEKS OF EXPERIMENTS IN MY HEAD.
I TRULY LOVE THIS WORK EVEN THOUGH I THINK IT MIGHT DESTROY ME.

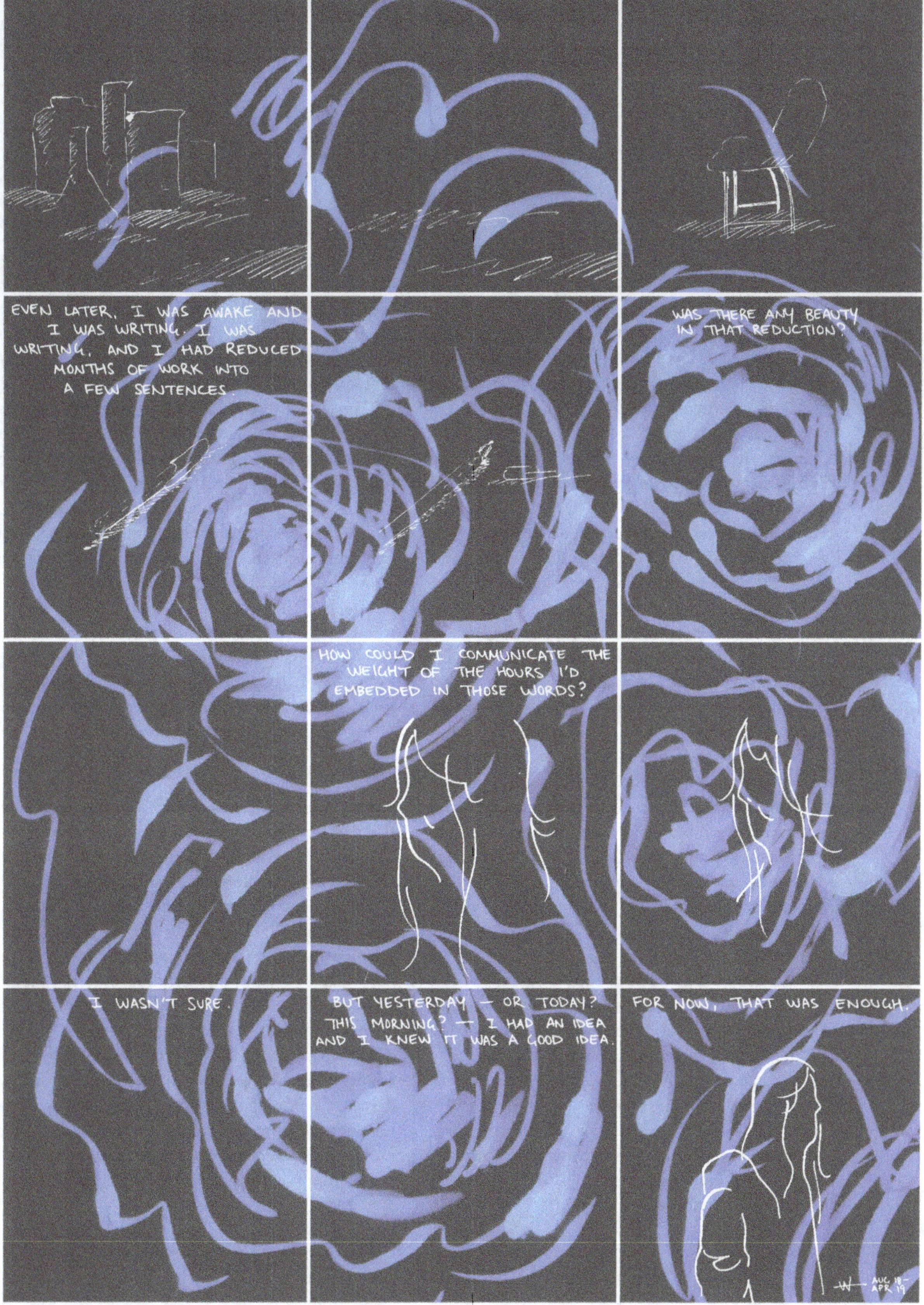
EVEN LATER, I WAS AWAKE AND I WAS WRITING. I WAS WRITING, AND I HAD REDUCED MONTHS OF WORK INTO A FEW SENTENCES.
WAS THERE ANY BEAUTY IN THAT REDUCTION?
HOW COULD I COMMUNICATE THE WEIGHT OF THE HOURS I'D EMBEDDED IN THOSE WORDS?
I WASN'T SURE.
BUT YESTERDAY — OR TODAY? THIS MORNING? — I HAD AN IDEA AND I KNEW IT WAS A GOOD IDEA.
FOR NOW, THAT WAS ENOUGH.

INTERVIEW

WITH ANDREW WHITE

When did you create "Impact"?

I drew the story in 2018 and 2019, working through several drafts of the piece with some time away from it between each draft. It originally appeared in the 2019 edition of my self-published comic *Yearly*.

What inspired this comic? Tell us more about the origins of its creation and whether any aspects of it were inspired by real life.

My wife works as a geneticist, and thanks to her I've come to some small understanding of the complex world of scientific research, including the people who make up that world. The main character of the comic is what's called a Principal Investigator—a professor at a university or other institution who runs their own research lab. I wanted to capture the feeling of working in this environment, which people often enter into at a fairly young age because of a genuine passion for science—but it's also an environment that can challenge or even destroy that passion. The title, "Impact," is a reference to the "impact factor" of a scientific journal (a measure of how often the papers in that journal are cited, seen as a proxy for the journal's quality), but also alludes to the broader idea of how we each define what it means to lead an "impactful" life.

How do you outline or draft your comics?

As some of your readers might know, the comics medium presents significant obstacles to working in drafts. For many cartoonists, drawing a single page can take many days. In addition, the important role played by page turns and panel layouts means that revising a single panel might in fact call for redrawing or resequencing an entire page or spread, for instance if that revised panel is a different size. Traditionally, the preferred solution to this conundrum has been to draft a story in sketches or layouts, but there's often a significant distance between the appearance of these layouts and the final pages of a comic. So that option isn't ideal, at least for me.

Instead, I've come to an approach that addresses these obstacles using two main tools. First, I generally draw in a loose, fairly sparse style that lets me produce drawings quickly and therefore more comfortably work through multiple finished drafts. As a result I usually skip the layout phase and begin directly with final pages. Second, I often work in grids, such as the twelve panel layout you see in "Impact." When all panels are the same size, I can more comfortably move images to different panels or pages without any unnecessary redrawing. There are disadvantages to this approach; for instance, my style wouldn't lend itself well to a story that calls for complex environments rendered in great detail. Still, it lets me work iteratively and intuitively.

These pages are beautifully rendered, blurring the lines between panels and overall layout. Was this an idea you had going into the comic, or something that came out organically?

The full-color background images for the comic are inspired by the fluorescent images of cells in scientific papers in genetics and cell biology, and in particular by images of Caenorhabditis elegans cells from my wife's doctoral thesis. I found these images breathtakingly beautiful, so the origin of "Impact" was my desire to make them the central feature of a comic. After a few experiments, I found that my own drawings capturing the spirit of these images worked better than the images themselves, since this gave me more control over the color scheme and exactly how much empty space appeared in the image.

Talk to me about the rhythm and pacing of your writing. Some panels in "Impact" are left blank, carried by the background art and sense of pacing. How do you decide which panels to leave empty?

This is difficult to describe, because it's a very inexact and intuitive process. I did know that the background images would play a key role in the piece, so I didn't want them to completely disappear behind dense foreground drawings. Beyond that, I can only say that I sequenced and resequenced the panels many times, adding or removing images and clumsily moving towards a layout that felt right.

Could you speak a bit about how you created the art in "Impact"? How much of this was done digitally?

The backgrounds of the comic were drawn with marker on tracing paper, and the linework was drawn straight to ink. I inverted the marker drawings digitally, which I found was the best way to replicate the neon colors of the images that inspired them. I also worked digitally to combine the two sets of drawings and iterate through drafts of the sequencing.

Your piece makes wonderful use of first person narration. What are the advantages and disadvantages in telling a story through this character's intimate monologue?

It's a delicate balance, especially in comics when the choice isn't only between first and third person narration but a question of whether to include narrative captions at all. In this case, I hope the narration accentuates the character's feelings of isolation and separation. Narration also appeals to me as a tool for allowing the imagery of a comic to become more tonal and even abstract at times.

Transitioning from creating artwork to fully-fledged comics can often feel daunting for artists. Do you have any tips for aspiring comic writers? What were things you wish you would have known when you were starting out?

This is a common piece of advice, but only because it's true: start with short stories. A simple mood or a quiet moment can be more than enough material for a 2-5 page comic, and that's a great length to focus on when you're starting out. Beyond that, especially for *Driftwood* readers who might come from a prose or poetry background, I'd underscore the importance of images to a comic and emphasize the fact that images shouldn't simply illustrate or restate the ideas communicated by the text of a comic.

Where can our readers find more of your work? Have you been published before?

Right now, my primary project is an annual self-published series called *Yearly* that I've notionally committed to publishing each year until I die. Since I started this project in 2018, I've been pleased by the way it has served as an organizing principle for my artistic practice and I've been surprised by the fact that the format of the final publication has often been different from one year to the next. You can order issues of *Yearly* directly from me or from comics retailers such as *Domino Books* and *Copacetic Comics*. Two recent book length works that might appeal to someone unfamiliar with my comics are *Ways to Survive in the Wilderness,* a poetic piece about climate change and community, and *Letters I'll Send Tomorrow*, a collection of short stories. These books are both available from most online retailers, and readers can see more of my work on my website (whitecomics.co).

Winter

by Kimball Anderson

I wake up in the dark

and let it stay with me throughout the day

in twisting and knotting branches

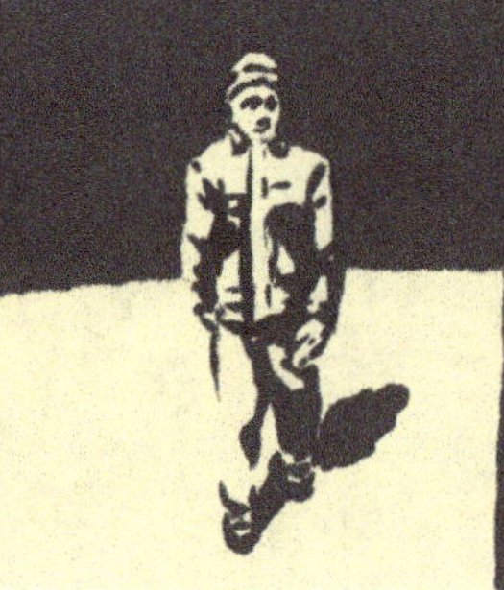

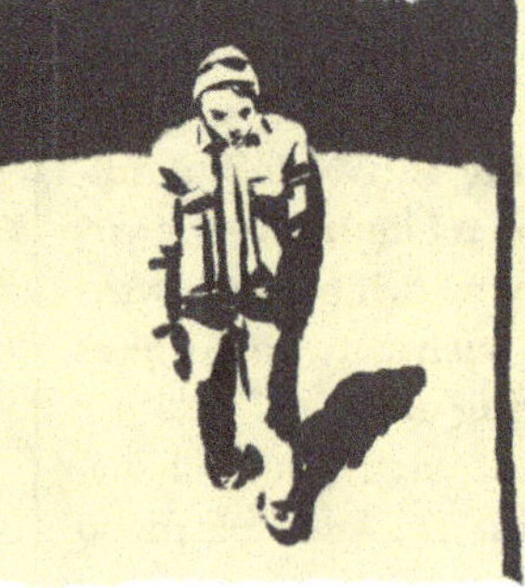

in the shadow under my feet

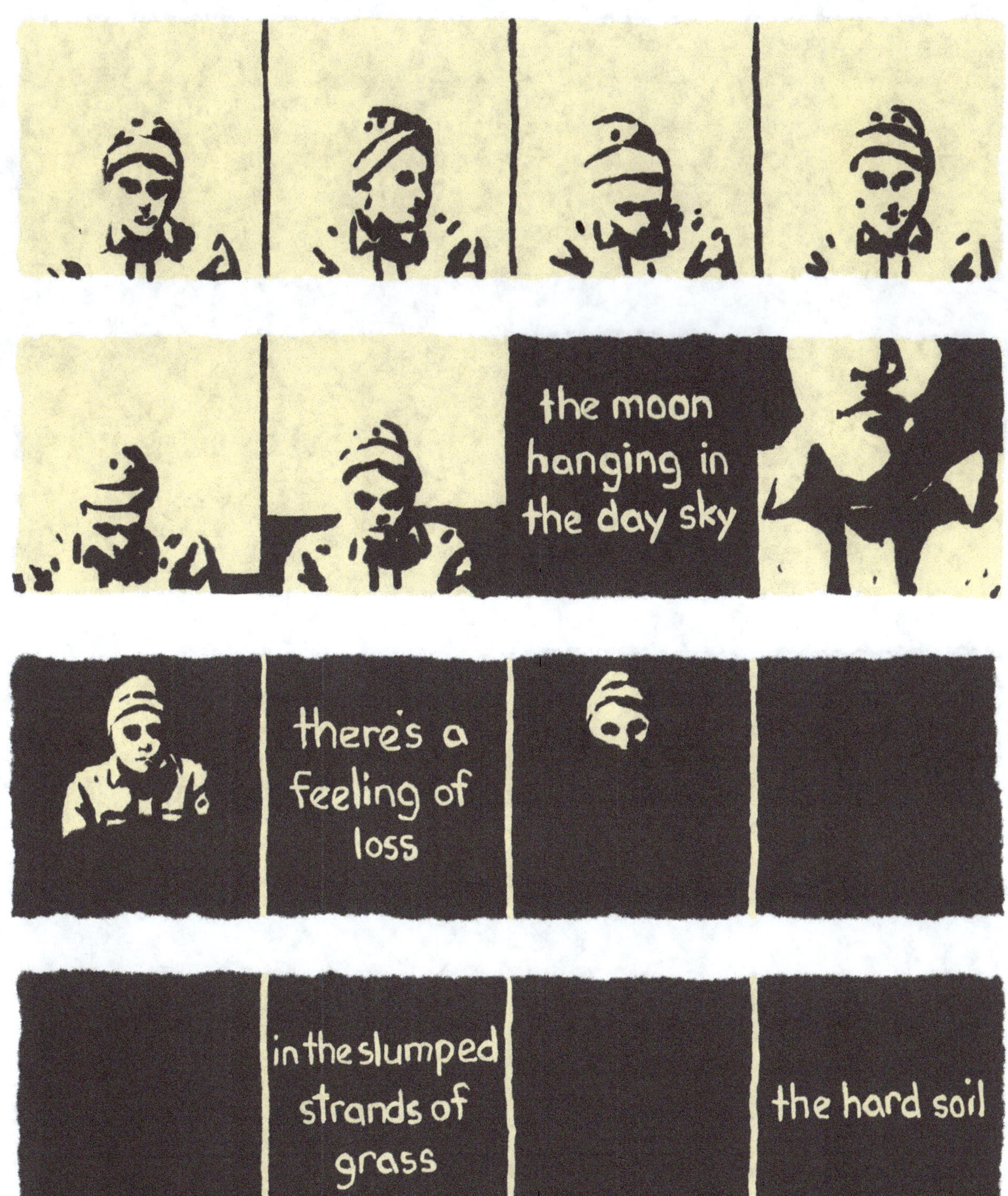

the moon
hanging in
the day sky
there's a
feeling of
loss
in the slumped
strands of
grass
the hard soil

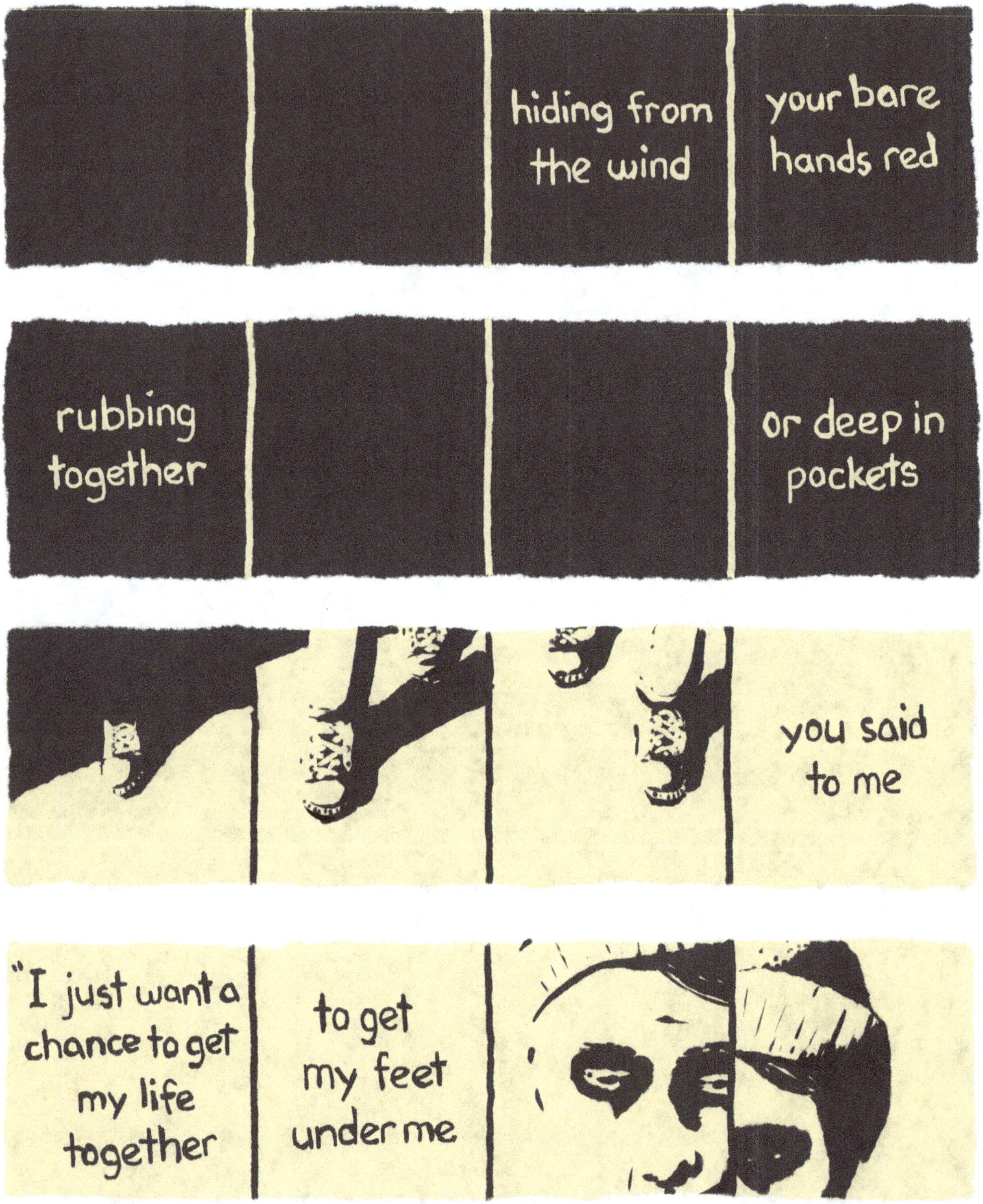

hiding from the wind

your bare hands red

rubbing together

or deep in pockets

you said to me

"I just want a chance to get my life together

to get my feet under me

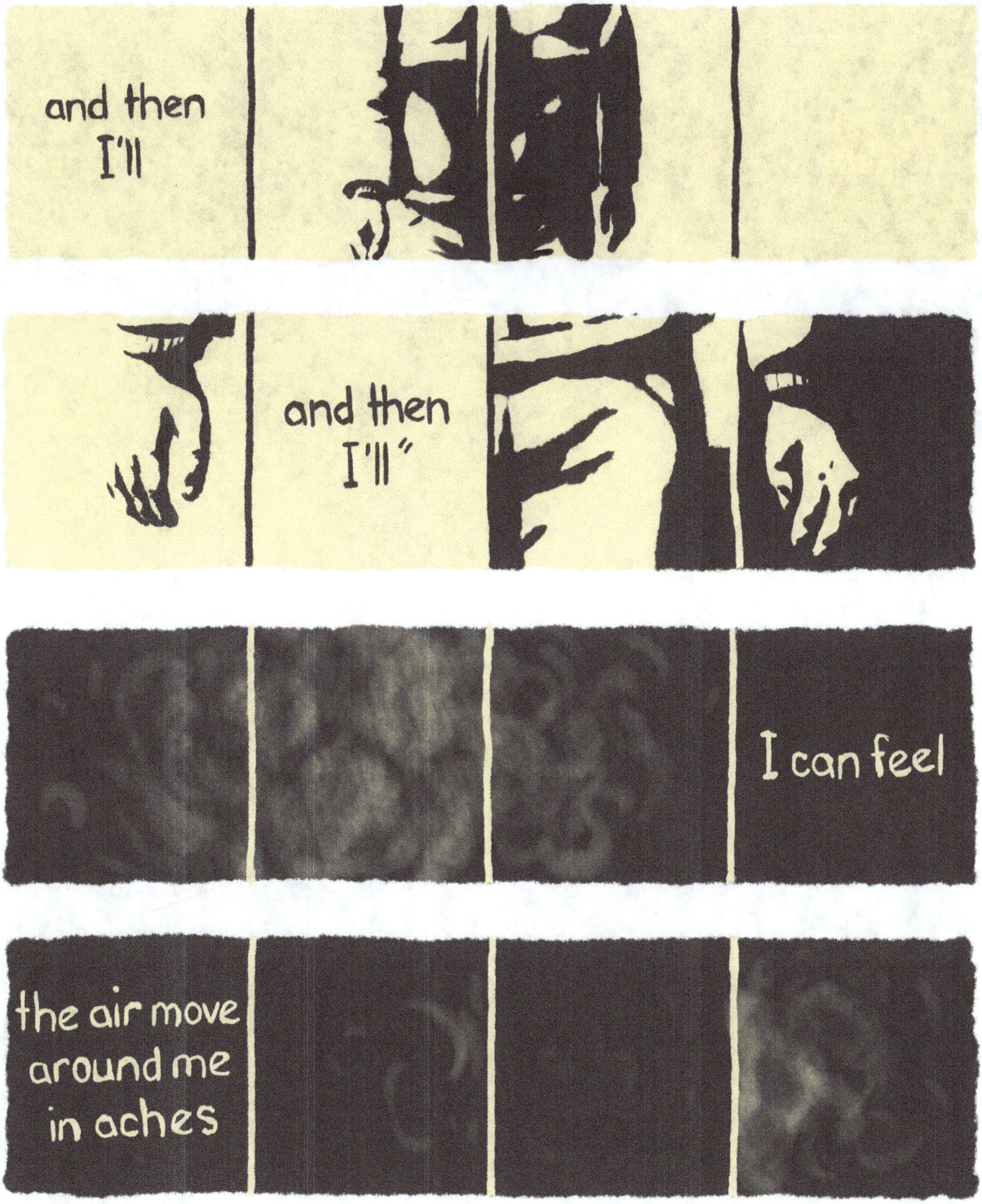

and then I'll

and then I'll"

I can feel

the air move around me in aches

across my skin

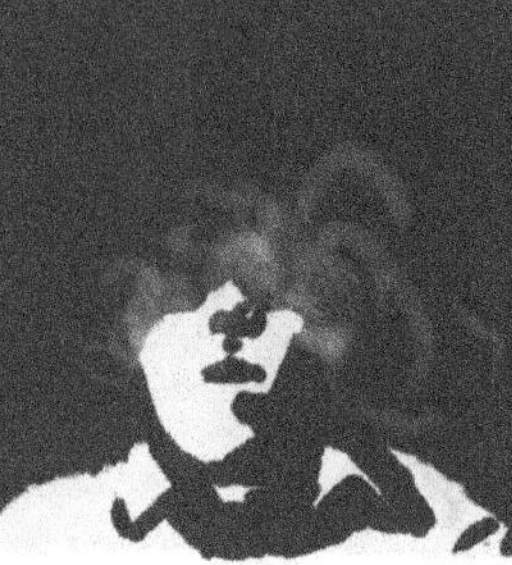

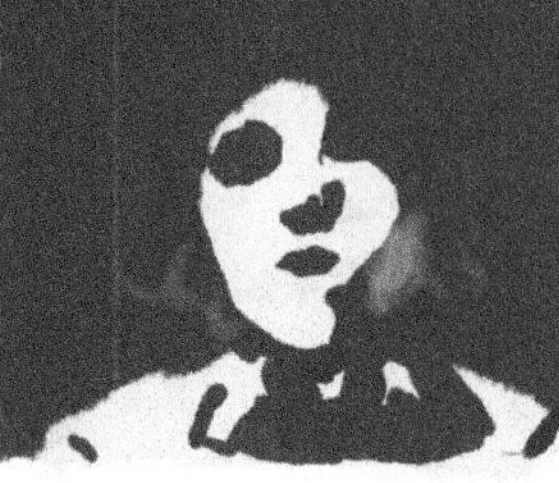

cracking and splitting

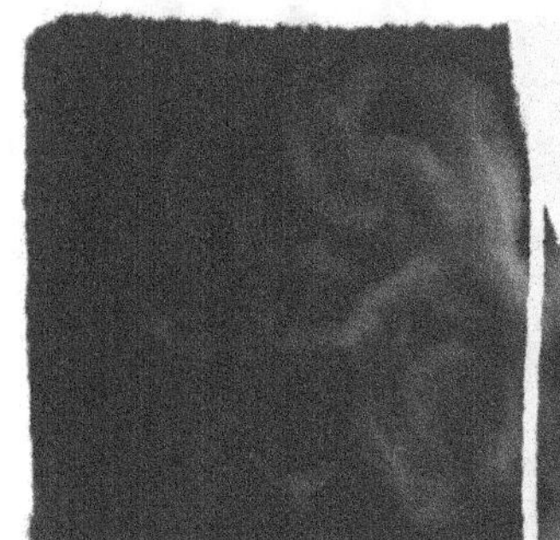

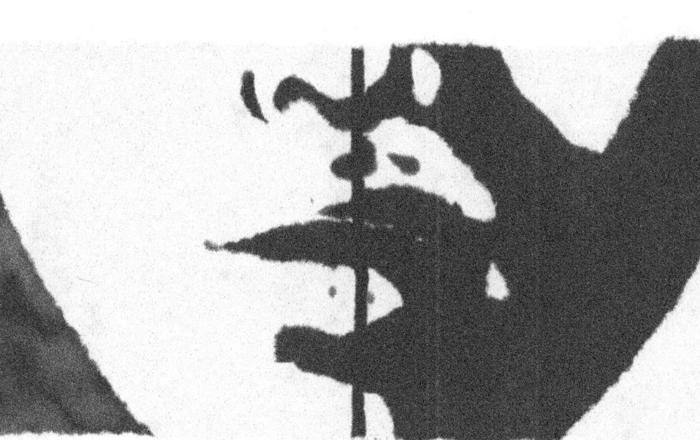

giving way to something rawer

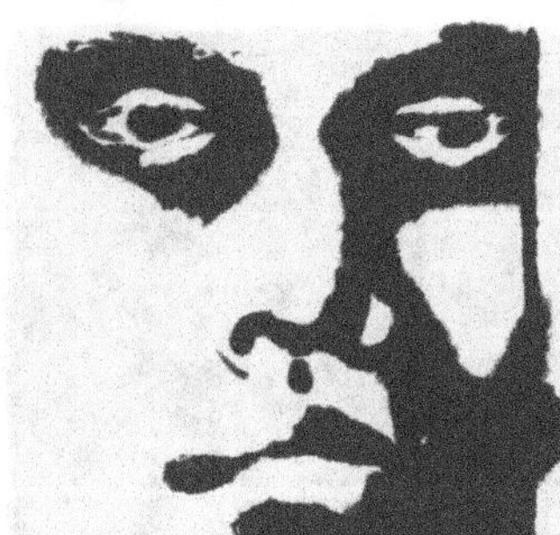

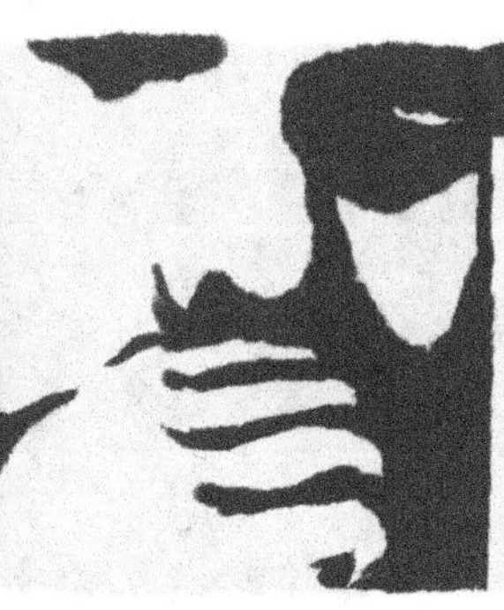

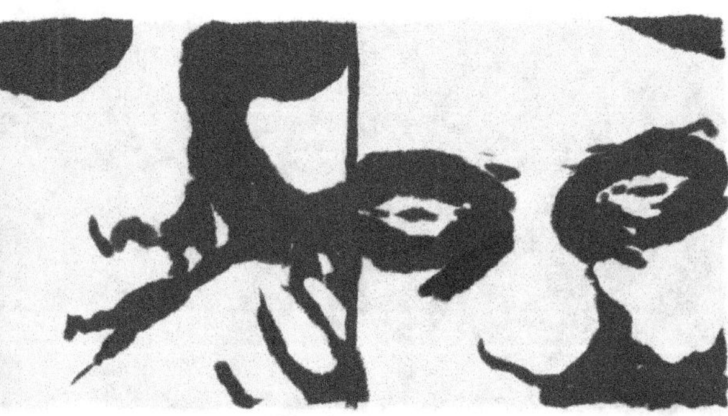

"do you remember when we were kids"

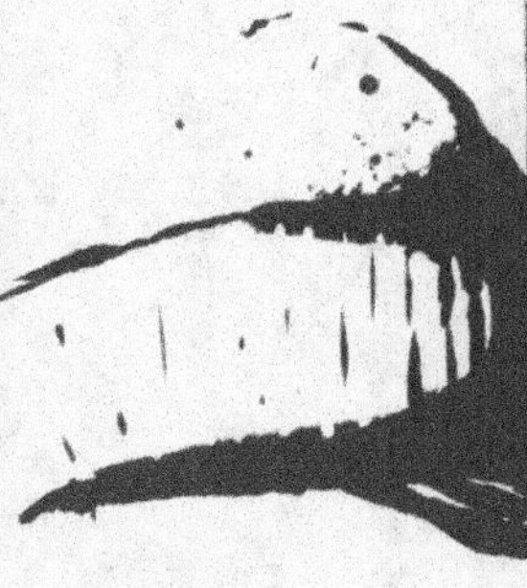

you asked me

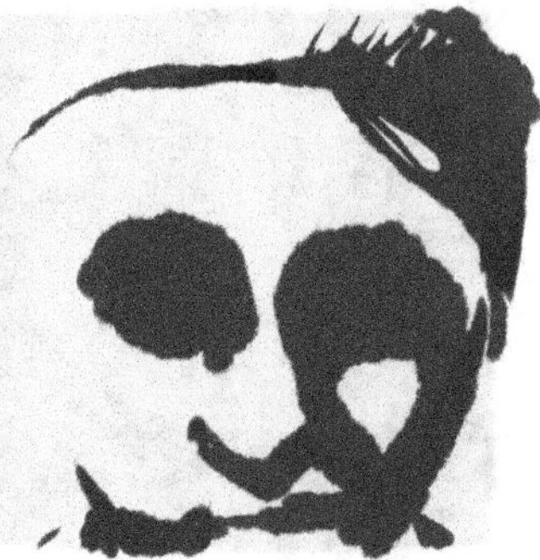

"and you always had a thermos of hot chocolate

and you'd let me have some

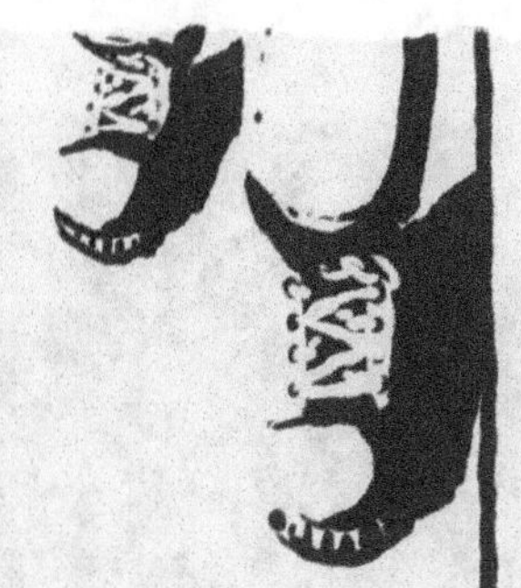

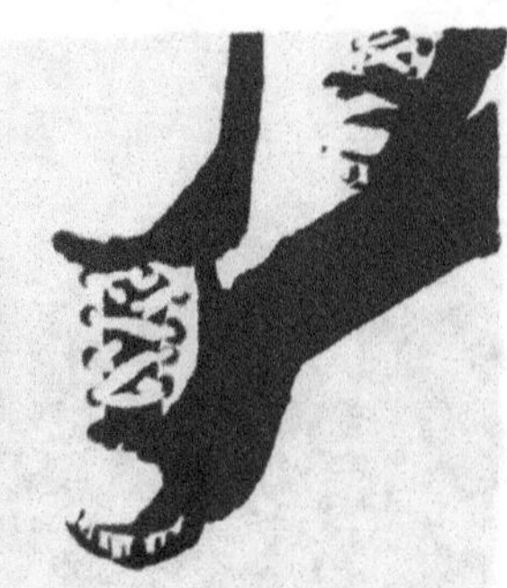

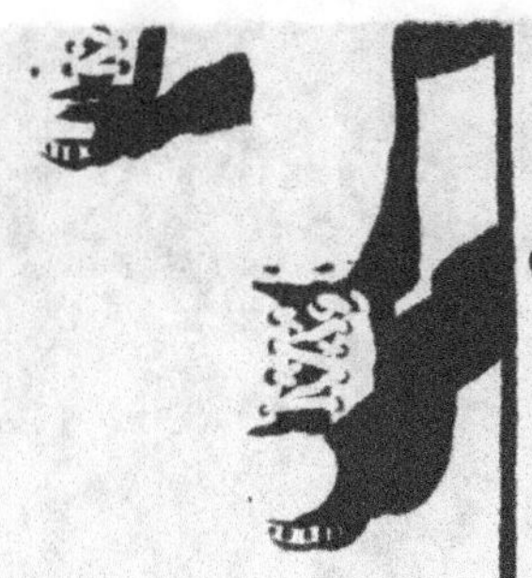

and it always felt so

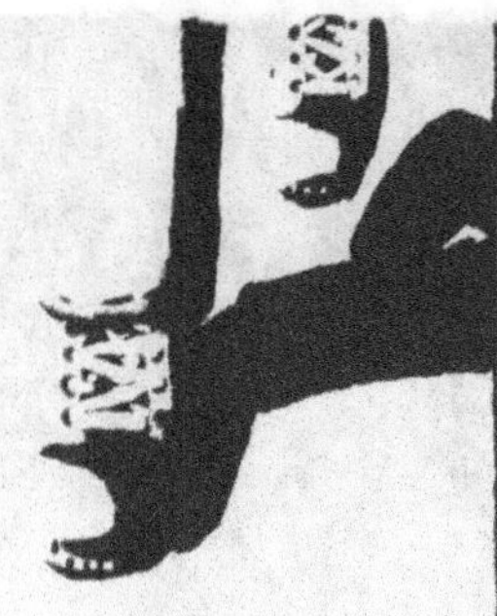

so special

that you'd share it with me

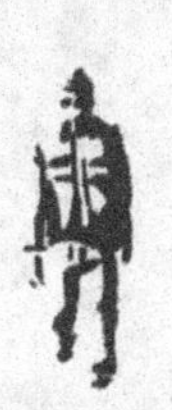

that I was worth it"

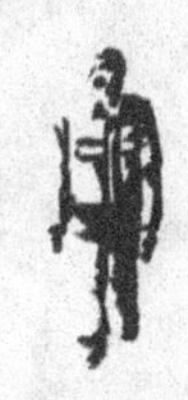

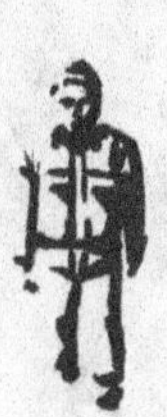

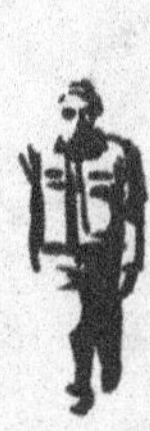

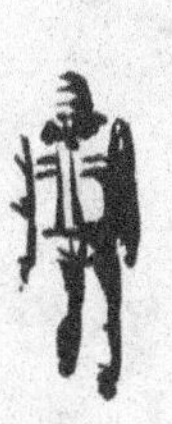

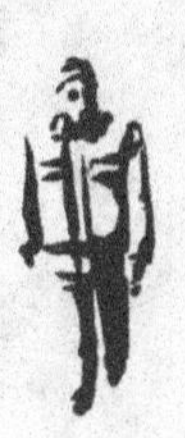

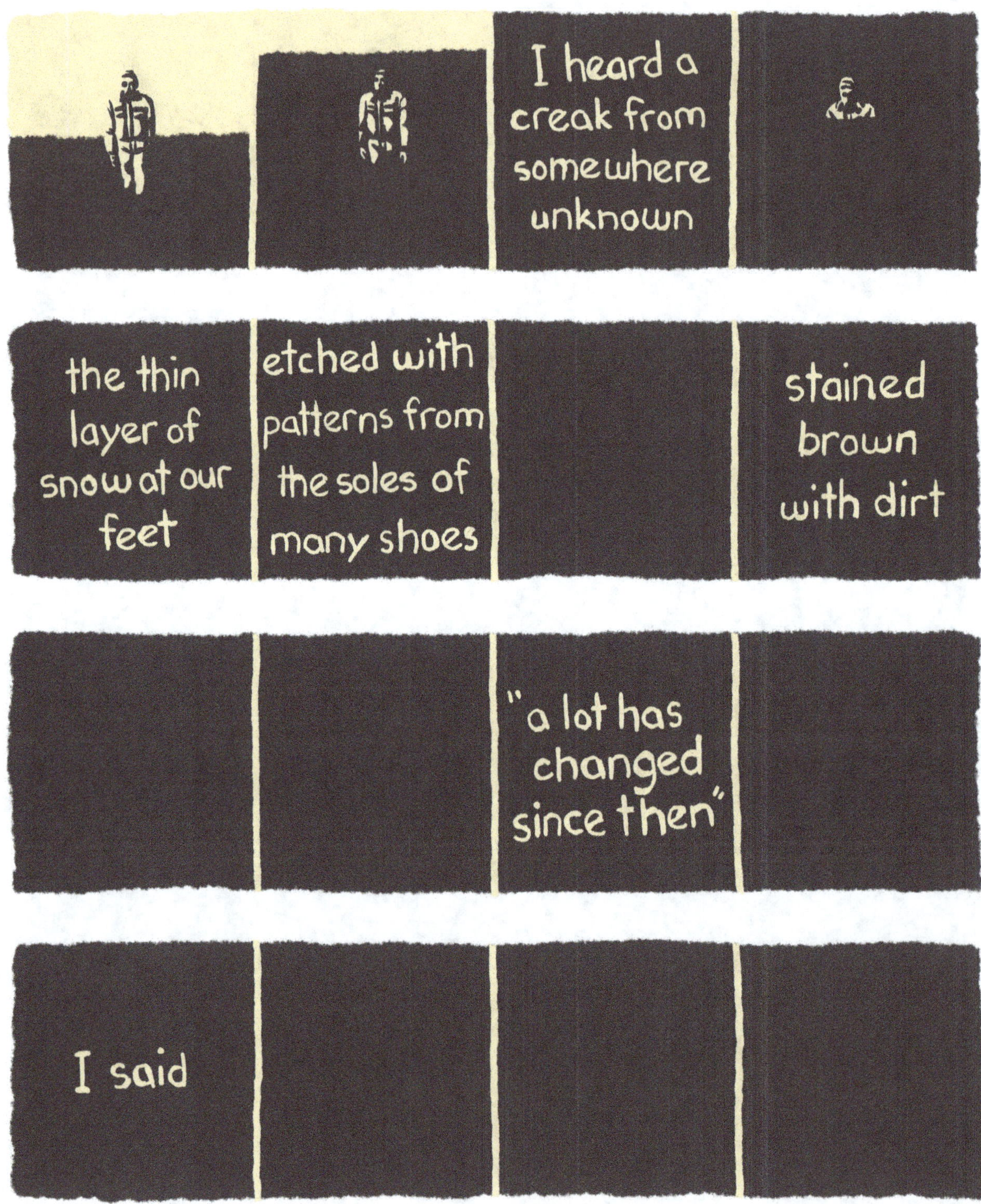
I heard a creak from somewhere unknown
the thin layer of snow at our feet
etched with patterns from the soles of many shoes
stained brown with dirt
"a lot has changed since then"
I said

INTERVIEW

WITH KIMBALL ANDERSON

How would you describe your aesthetic?

A friend of mine just said of a comic I made that it was "tender but deals with big things." I was like, *Oh yeah, that's kind of my thing, isn't it?* The way my hands make marks and the way I write stories is gentle I guess. So much of what we value in art is boldness, and I get that, but boldness simplifies. I want to find all of the complexity and subtlety in the smallest things in life and the emotions that drive us.

When creating a comic, what are your biggest visual goals? What do you like to emphasize?

I tend to want to tailor the visual style of the comic entirely around the theme or sensation I'm trying to communicate. Sometimes I'll do a photo comic if I feel like that will communicate the idea better, or get a lot scribblier with my art. I think we often think of style as an artist's identity, that they only have this one "voice." And we end up limiting the full capacity for expression. I feel like the most important thing is the message, and the format of the message is in service to that.

Your piece makes use of a limited but gorgeous color palette. How did you land on these colors?

I had this image in my mind of someone walking in the dark under street lights. At night, when you see someone appear from under a street light, they look bright and yellow. I could have done a pure black, but I think that doesn't get across the feeling as well... There's a sort of murkiness to night vision that black is too solid to communicate. A warm charcoal fits the feeling better.

Similarly, the paneling structure is standardized but communicates a nearly haunting winter aesthetic. When you are planning a comic, how do you decide on a layout?

Yeah, that's what's cool about standardized layouts! It's an underlying steady rhythm, which I think really pairs well with the bleakness of winter. I wanted to have that sort of plodding through the cold feeling, where you are more aware of each step because your senses won't allow your mind to drift off. So, each panel is regular like each step is regular.

The temporal element of comics is weird, because obviously anyone can read through comics at any speed they like. But often a larger panel can feel like a "breath," like you take a moment more to just take in what's in it. And a smaller panel is read at a more rapid pace, which might track each step of a complex motion or a quick exchange. So if all the panels are the same size and shape, they are read in the same way and at the same pace!

To your mind, what are some of the benefits and disadvantages of internal narration leading the writing as opposed to concrete scenes? Talk to me a little about your narration style.

I wrote the text for this first as a sort of poem, and then adapted it into a comic form. When you are adapting like this, the choice of imagery can deepen the meaning or make everything feel more shallow.

I guess I never thought about it as internal narration or any other sort of specific narration. It was more like, what juxtaposition will add more meaning to the words. And maybe the implication is that this character is thinking this, or feeling this, but I like it better as an undefined implicit idea.

We'd call this a poetry comic. How would you categorize it?

This is definitely a poetry comic! But poetry comics are interesting because they don't have to be like this—where the words by themselves would be a sort of poem. They can be wordless, using the imagery in the same way other poets use words. Pared down to the most delicate and precise meaning, trying to chart the space around the ineffable. And in that way, this comic as just the words would not contain the same sort of feeling or meaning to me.

What other mediums have influenced your work? How?

Ugh, it's embarrassing, but I have been really influenced by TV shows. I got sick young and one of the main things I could do to rest was to watch TV, so I'd watch like fifteen hours a day most days. And in my brainfogged mind, it all became a confused jumble of images and ideas that I couldn't really place. This was sort of a backwards influence though, because the things that were lacking from that TV world were what I became more interested in. I'd rather see that car ride home that they skipped over—between the climax and the wrap up. Or like Don Draper looking at the fly caught in the fluorescent light and feeling some unknown feeling. What if that was the whole show?

Since my teens, I definitely have had more influences. Differentiated repetition is really cool, and so is visual poetry. Experimental and discordant music probably helped me understand how to play with expectations of rhythm. I think this also helped me understand how to experiment with narrative without losing the plot.

You use space in such a vivid and interesting way. What was the process like in deciding which panels would hold what?

I think it's mostly instinctual and based on creating a rhythm between panels. Panels are both space and time in the experience of reading a comic, so it's a matter of composition of an art piece as well as a matter of composing a narrative structure. The nice thing about poetry comics is that you have less narrative necessities in what you show. You don't have to figure out how to draw "and the character picks up the bus ticket, opens the door, and walks out" as three panels. You are able to let the scene breathe more and be about guiding the reader through a feeling.

Transitioning from creating artwork to fully-fledged comics can often feel daunting for artists. Do you have any tips for aspiring comic writers? What were things you wish you would have known when you were starting out?

If you are an artist interested in this sort of work, I think an interesting way to approach it would be to start slow and just add text into your art. Create one page comics out of what would have been just drawings or paintings, and see how the words bounce off of the images. If you like that, make a bunch, until you've explored everything you can think to say in the space. I found this very freeing and fun, myself, but at some point I started to feel like the ambiguity I could explore between words and images started to feel the same. At that point, expand. With more pages you can create specificity to play off of. Figure out what means something to you to communicate—and what tools you can use to create that!

I feel like this is a fun way to do things because it's just playing around and feeling your way through. Even if you have a big idea for the comic you want to create, playing around is key. It's so easy to fall into the trap of thinking this next project has to be great and perfect, then psyche yourself out. Letting yourself play around can help you avoid this!

What are your own artistic goals for the future? Simply, what do you want to do next?

I want to collaborate with people more! I have a couple of collaborations with friends that I've had in some form of stasis for too long. It would be nice if one of those really happened. There's something beautiful to me about the idea of it. Maybe I'm just jealous of people in bands who get to have jam sessions.

"STRANGERS"

BY CASEY JO STOHRER

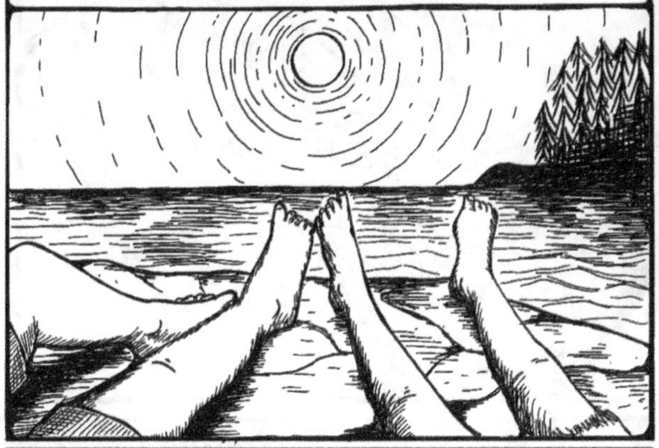

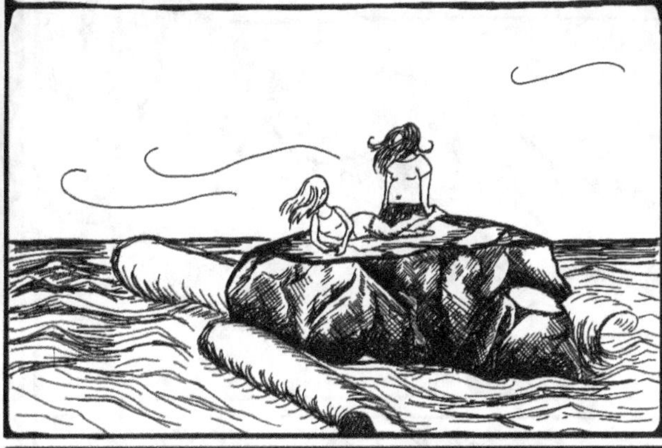

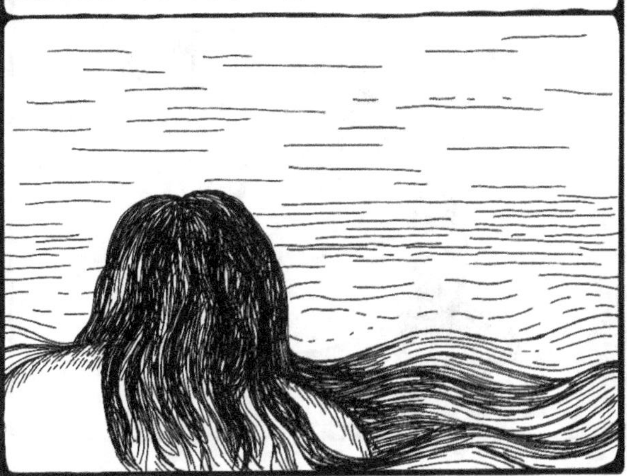

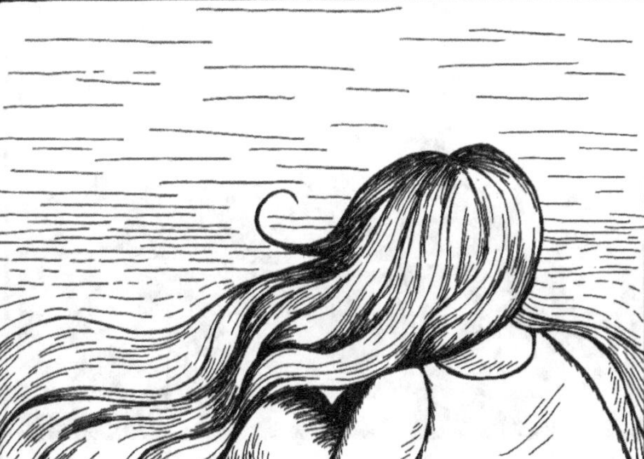

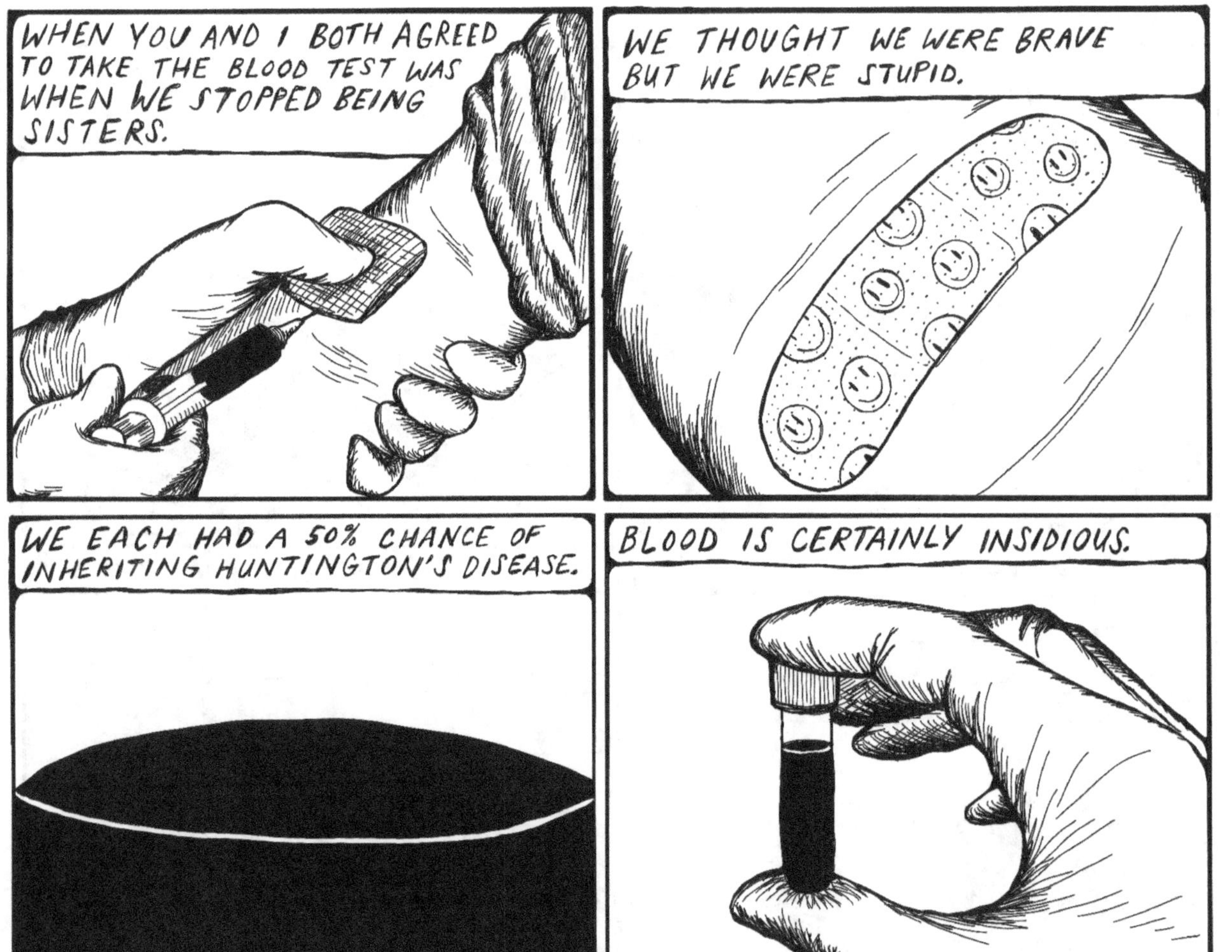
WHEN YOU AND I BOTH AGREED TO TAKE THE BLOOD TEST WAS WHEN WE STOPPED BEING SISTERS.
WE THOUGHT WE WERE BRAVE BUT WE WERE STUPID.
WE EACH HAD A 50% CHANCE OF INHERITING HUNTINGTON'S DISEASE.
BLOOD IS CERTAINLY INSIDIOUS.

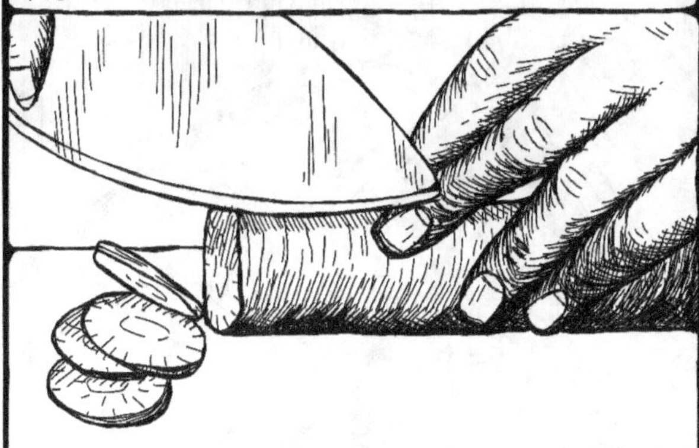
WE ARE SEPARATED FROM IT BY MERE MILLIMETERS...

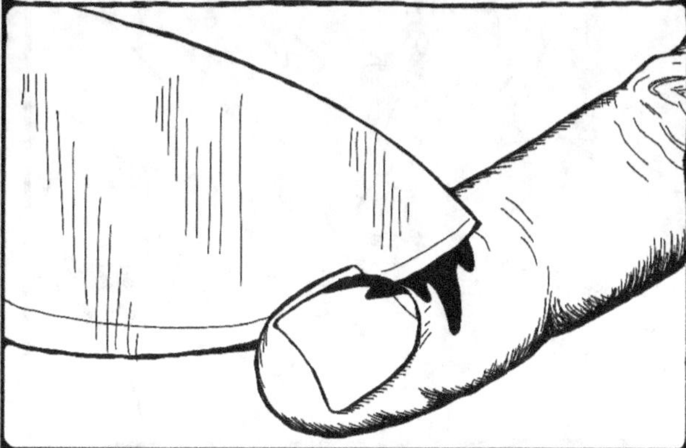
...A WILD UNDERCURRENT SHIELDED BY AVERAGE SKIN, COMFORTABLE REALITY.

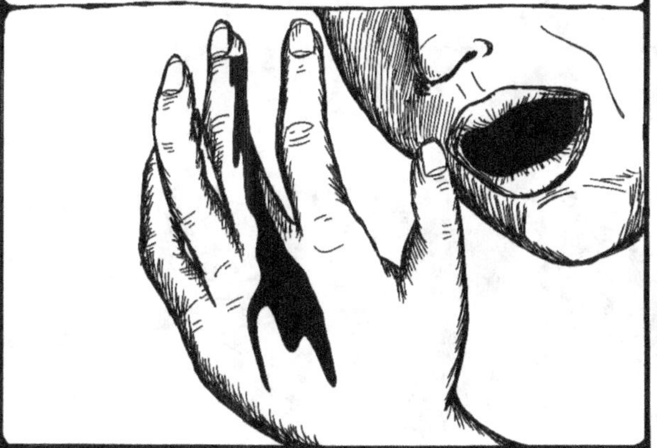
WHEN WE COME FACE TO FACE WITH IT, IT DISTURBS US LIKE A STRANGER.

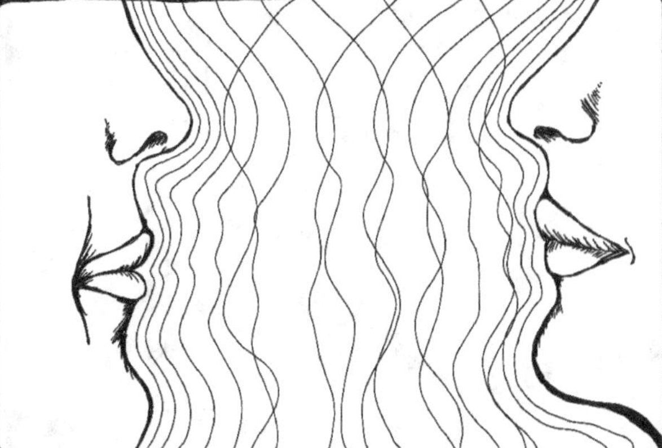
I NEVER THOUGHT WE'D BECOME ESTRANGED BY SUCH A CONSEQUENCE.

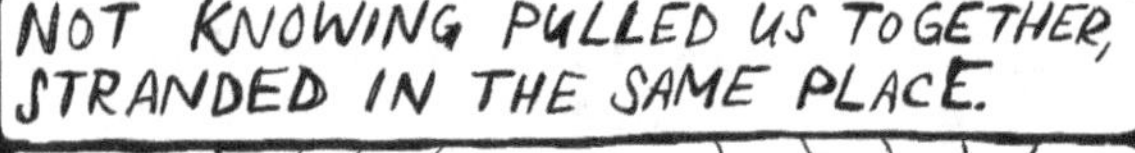

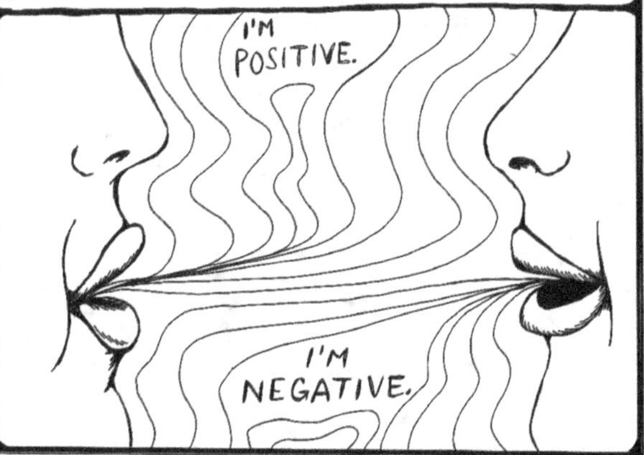

GETTING THE RESULTS PUSHED US MILES AWAY.

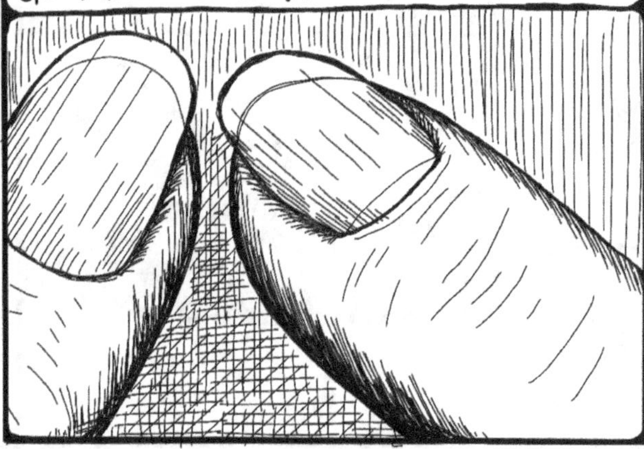

WHAT WOULD OUR LIVES HAVE BEEN LIKE IF WE HAD JUST KEPT ON BELIEVING

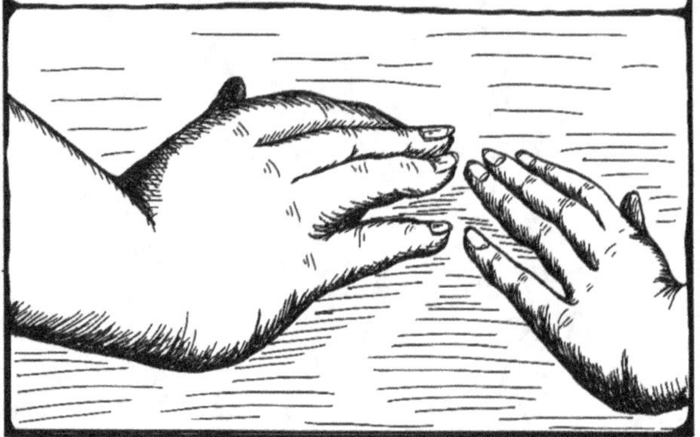

IN A POSSIBILITY TOGETHER INSTEAD OF KNOWING THE TRUTH APART?

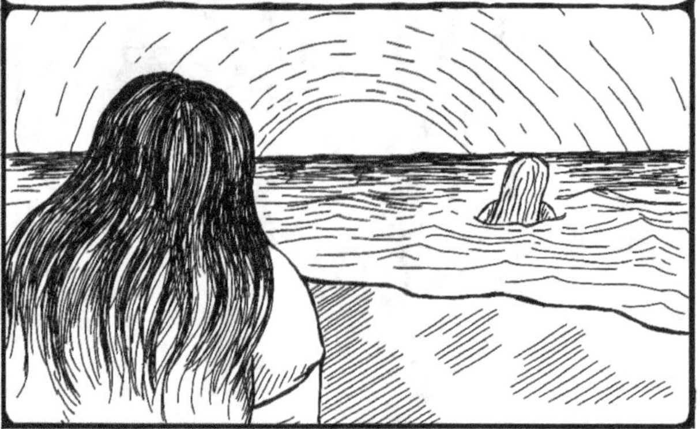

Casey Jo '19

INTERVIEW

WITH CASEY JO STOHRER

How would you describe your aesthetic?

Space-grunge. Gritty and stark.

Did you have a difficult time deciding on whether to add a title to your work?

Always. I went through a few versions and different titles trying to sum it up efficiently.

When did you create "Strangers"?

A few years ago, my sister and I decided to get genetic testing done. Our dad has Huntington's Disease, which exhibits a really harrowing and bizarre mix of symptoms. It is a rare degenerative neurological disease that is also hereditary. Children of HD-positive people have a 50/50 chance of inheriting it. My dad used to describe it as bipolar disorder, Alzheimer's, Tourette's, schizophrenia, and Parkinson's all wrapped up into one. It was important to my sister and me to get our genetic make-up revealed to us, so we could plan our futures accordingly. The genetic testing for this disease is incredibly intense, involving mandatory mental health counseling beforehand so the doctors could even determine if we were mentally sound enough to accept bad news. In a sense, it is a situation where you discover how you are going to die.

What was the hardest part of crafting the piece?

I have written and drawn a lot about this topic, and there are so many dimensions to it that it can be hard to narrow down a theme. To describe dissociation or isolation is one of the main motivations that people create, but to really hone in on the nuances of this particular subject was difficult.

Was there any theme or idea you hoped to address with this work?

The whole "ignorance is bliss" argument has always been a concept that fascinated me. Can people succeed (or even just function) in life living with these great looming mysteries? Or is it better to know? My whole life, I've lived with this detrimental mystery, and the answer was, quite literally, physically in me. This inner spectre started to drive me crazy after awhile. A real-life Schrodinger's paradox. Did I want to open that box? What would my life be like if I knew how I was (likely) going to go out?

When creating a comic, what are your biggest visual goals? What do you like to emphasize?

The past few years, I've had this fascination of capturing these fuzzy, up-close, little moments and flashes of memory. A lot of comics emphasize movement and fluidity. I've always had a process of drawing very slowly, almost like sculpting—just chipping away at my lines and drawing and re-tracing until I get the picture that I want, usually with a lot of detail. This goes against the basic tenets of traditional comics, where images should be quick and elastic. I want the images to stand very solid on the page. I feel like the movement comes more into play with the words (where I tend to be more abstract) and the images are anchoring them into reality.

Similarly, what are your biggest narrative concerns?

I am often guilty of being too vague or abstract—in attempts of trying to catch all of these other thoughts and meanings. The challenge is narrowing down the messages with the correct images.

What instruments did you use here?

I pretty much have only used the dry ink pen in Procreate for iPad for most of my recent work, though for this story I used a studio ink pen. I love working with pencils and charcoals, and the digital pens specifically have the malleability I like. I felt guilty for a long time, doing drawings exclusively on the iPad and not using "real life" materials, but it has also allowed me to experiment and edit quicker than I could using traditional materials.

How do you outline or draft your comics?

For the most part, the "script" comes first. I like working with panels of equal size within a grid. It allows me to break down the words into neat little sections, and I can change their positions easily if needed. I usually get the grid established and write my script within each panel, then do a quick sketch of the action just to get the story down. Then I go back and trace the outlines and add details.

Considering the story leans on narration, did you find yourself creating the images first, or did the writing happen before you drew anything?

The writing usually comes first. I did recently complete a comic where the images came first, and then the words, which was a great change-up of process for that particular story. I drew some free-association panels regarding the topic, and then I arranged them as I wrote the script.

What can comics uniquely communicate about illness and disease narratives that other mediums cannot?

There are both words and images to describe a feeling or action, which can be overkill sometimes, but it can also open up myriad combinations of thoughts and allow for a certain amount of abstraction, while still being grounded. The clinical, dry realities of dealing with a disease are a dramatically different outer world pushing right up against the emotionally disparate inner world. I always found hospitals so strange in that doctors and nurses are dealing with science, with facts and information totally separate from human emotion and experience, yet they are directly responsible for the emotional well-being of patients as well as their physical well-being. In hospitals, people experience explosions of emotion within themselves against the white jackets and brick walls and fluorescent lights, against facts and realities that have nothing to do with emotion. These two worlds seem to work against each other even though they are two sides of the same coin. The same can be said with images and text.

Is this fictionalized or nonfiction? If the latter, did the relationship improve?

This is purely non-fiction, down to the bone. My sister and I did not talk for about four years after we found out our test results. There were other issues involved, and I wouldn't blame the genetic testing entirely for this rift, but it was definitely a part of it. We recently started talking again, and it's been good so far. There are just some things I will never experience or understand that my sister will, and it hurts knowing we are forever disconnected in this way. We are learning how to reckon with this information and accept it.

This comic was initially submitted as a sixteen-panel page. Unfortunately, we had to split it up into four panels per page to fit the comic in our issue. Was anything lost or gained in this transition? Do you consider publication or printing when crafting your comics?

Splitting up in fours was actually great, as I thought of these panels in groups of four. Ideally I'd like the whole story to fit on one page, but printed presentation allows me to really edit it down to the essentials. I try to have the images flow as a whole, and then break them up into little subsets of ideas/concepts if needed.

What other comic mediums do you work in? Do you have a particular preference?

Lately, I've been doing these serious autobiographical comics to help me organize my past. But I also like to do weird and darkly humorous stories, usually about fictional creatures or creature-y humans. I feel like these two sides don't always align into a singular style. I don't know if that is an issue I should address eventually. Most days I say "fuck it" and let the various styles take their own shape and tone, because who gives a shit?

Transitioning from creating artwork to fully-fledged comics can often feel daunting for artists. Do you have any tips for aspiring comic writers? What were things you wish you would have known when you were starting out?

I always loved writing and drawing separately, so it seemed like a natural transition to get into this medium. I am still working on my issues of speed and minimizing the details, which have always bogged me down. Doing small details can become obsessive and unnecessary, especially with digital processes where the possibilities are endless. I constantly revise and edit. I believe that style comes from what you take away, and what is left on the page. My advice is to be open to outside criticism from people you trust, and of course yourself, and do not be afraid of revising. Look at editing as an equally creative part of the process, along with getting the original ideas down.

When does a comic feel "done" in your mind?

Usually, once all the panels are completed, I will mix and match words and images and rearrange the panels until the message "clicks" into place. Once I can see the flow that I want, then I know it's complete.

If you had to narrow it down, who would you say are your three biggest influences?

Right now, I am a huge fan of E. A. Bethea; they are distributed by a small publisher called *Domino Books*. Bethea's style is very stream of consciousness and takes surface objects and imagery and dives deep with poetry that is often emotionally hilarious. I also like the psychedelic absurdity of Olivier Schrauwen's comics. Noah van Sciver is another artist that does these great autobiographical comics. I relate to his work a lot, maybe because we are from the same town in NJ. When I was a kid, I read the Sunday funnies religiously. *Calvin and Hobbes* was my favorite. The art of a four panel action-and-punchline trope might seem corny or lowbrow to some people, but to produce a comic every week that upholds the same small structure—and to do it consistently well—is an incredible feat.

What other mediums have influenced your work? How?

Music and painting have been a huge influence on me all my life. My dad was a passionate music listener, the only non-musician I knew that could describe music better than anyone who ever picked up an instrument. He was a drunk and into jazz at the time. He'd disappear on benders and leave us with Charlie Parker, Miles Davis, and Coltrane. Storytelling, rhythm, and flow are important to any medium regardless of the execution. I got to understand the concepts of motifs through jazz music, of point and counterpoint, even if I didn't formally know what those terms meant at the time. My mom educated me on art and design history, and we practically lived at the Philadelphia Art Museum when I was growing up. Surrealism has probably had the most impact directly on my comics; the use of literal symbols to express an intangible feeling or idea is my bread and butter. I don't really care if that's not cool anymore. Signifiers are fascinating.

Where can our readers find more of your work? Have you been published before?

I have been published in *The Lincoln Review* and *Spiralbound on Medium*, and I am a semi-regular contributor to a local Nashville zine called *The Salt Weekly*. In between freelancing and day job work, I am slowly compiling a collection of autobiographical pieces to self-publish in the near future. For the most part, I just post my one-offs on my Instagram (@misscaseyjo).

What are your own artistic goals for the future? Simply, what do you want to do next?

I just want to quit my freaking job.

What drew you to *Driftwood Press*?

I had been following *Driftwood* for awhile, and the caliber of the works published soon amounted to me putting *Driftwood* as one of my "holy grail" quests.

Contributors

Rachel Phillippo writes from rural Indiana where she resides down a long "tree tunnel" lane along with her husband, five children, and an assortment of pets. She received her MFA in fiction from Spalding University's brief residency program. "Wing Breaker" is her first short story publication.

Dailihana Alfonseca is currently working on her Masters in Latino/a Studies with a focus on the cultural legacy of the African Diaspora and the marginalization of Caribbean Immigrants. She resides in South Carolina with her family and is a member of South Carolina Writers Association. Her writing reflects on the immigrant experience within America and the cultural trauma that is a result of what W.E.B. Dubois calls "Double Consciousness." Her poetry has previously appeared in *The Bangalore Review*. This is her first short story publication.

Laura Ohlmann is an MFA graduate from the University of Central Florida. Her work has appeared in *The Rumpus, Saw Palm, The Lindenwood Review, The Maine Review, GASHER, South Carolina Review, South Florida Poetry Journal,* and others. She's one of the Associate Editors of *West Trade Review*. She enjoys traveling in her converted Honda Element and biking up mountains with her partner and dog.

Niki Tulk is an ex-pat Australian writer and theater-maker. She has published poetry and fiction in *The Saranac Review Tenth Anniversary Edition, Rock River Review, The Sheepshead Review, The Feminist Wire, The Journal of Language and Literacy Education, West Trade Review* and *Southerly*. In 2018, her novella, *Before Rain,* was a finalist for the International Miami Book Fair / de Groot Prize, where it earned the recommendation of the judge, Jim Shepard. Niki holds an MFA from the New School.

Cynthia Bargar's poems have appeared in *Rogue Agent, Book of Matches, LUMINA, Stoneboat Literary Journal, Comstock Review,* and other journals. *Sleeping in the Dead Girl's Room*, in which "Other Cynthia" appears, is her debut collection coming out from *Lily Poetry Review Books* in 2022. Her prose poem, "Saint Mary's Beach," is included in a new book of images and text, *Our Provincetown: Intimate Portraits* by Barbara Cohen, published by *Provincetown Arts Press*. Cynthia is associate poetry editor at *Pangyrus LitMag*. She lives in Provincetown, Massachusetts.

Laura Rosenthal grew up in New York and lives in Sacramento, California. She received degrees from Cornell University and Stanford Law School and is about to enter Pacific University's MFA program in creative writing (poetry). Before returning to her first love, writing, she worked for several decades as a lawyer, focusing on access to health care and health insurance. She has been published in the anthology *Quiet Rooms, Boog City, Buddhist Poetry Review,* and other journals. She is a member of the Community of Writers and has been an editor of *Tule Review*.

Beth Suter studied Environmental Science at U.C. Davis and has worked as a naturalist and teacher. She is also a Pushcart Prize nominee. Her poems have appeared in *Colorado Review, Barrow Street, DMQ Review, Poet Lore*, and *Birmingham Poetry Review*, among others. She lives in California with her husband and son.

Kari Rueckert graduated with an MFA in Creative Writing at Eastern Washington University. She lives in Minneapolis, MN and loves to play with her dog Luna.

DALIAH ANGELIQUE is a lesbian poet chronicling memory, late stage capitalist hellscapes, and feminine rage. Her work has appeared in *Glass: A Journal of Poetry, The Poetry Society of New York,* and *Anti-Heroin Chic.* She lives in Washington state with her wife and chihuahua.

CAROLYN OLIVER is the author of *Inside the Storm I Want to Touch the Tremble* (*University of Utah Press,* forthcoming), selected by Matthew Olzmann for the Agha Shahid Ali Prize. Carolyn's poems appear in *The Massachusetts Review, Indiana Review, Cincinnati Review, Radar Poetry, Shenandoah, Beloit Poetry Journal, 32 Poems, Southern Indiana Review, Cherry Tree, Plume, DIALOGIST,* and elsewhere. Carolyn is the winner of the E.E. Cummings Prize from the NEPC, the Goldstein Prize from *Michigan Quarterly Review*, and the Writer's Block Prize in Poetry. Carolyn lives in Massachusetts with her family. You can find her online (carolynoliver.net).

SARA MOORE WAGNER is the winner of the 2021 *Cider Press Review* Editors Prize for her book *Swan Wife* (2022), and the 2020 *Driftwood Press* Poetry Collection Prize for *Hillbilly Madonna* (2022). She is also 2021 National Poetry Series Finalist, and the recipient of a 2019 Sustainable Arts Foundation award. Her poetry has appeared in many journals and anthologies including *Sixth Finch, Waxwing, Nimrod, Beloit Poetry Journal,* and *The Cincinnati Review,* among others. Find her online (www.saramoorewagner.com).

LAURA BANDY earned her MFA from the University of Illinois Urbana-Champaign in 2006 and attended the University of Southern Mississippi's Center for Writers PhD program from 2009 to 2013, where she received the Joan Johnson Poetry Award. In 2018, she won first prize in the "Trio of Triolets" contest judged by Allison Joseph, and received third place in the Gwendolyn Brooks Poetry Award/ Illinois Emerging Writers Competition that same year. Her chapbook, *Hack*, was published with *Dancing Girl Press* in summer 2021, and she has work forthcoming in *The Florida Review* and *Moist Poetry Journal.* Laura is a member of the English faculty at Spoon River Community College. She hails from Jacksonville, Illinois, home of the Ferris wheel.

HEATHER BARTLETT's work can be found in *Barrow Street, Carolina Quarterly, Lambda Literary, Los Angeles Review, Ninth Letter, Redivider, RHINO Poetry,* and other journals. Her chapbook, *Bleeding Yellow Light* was published by *From Yes Press* in 2009. She is a professor of English and Creative Writing at the State University of New York at Cortland and editor of the online literary magazine, *Hoxie Gorge Review.*

CHRISTINE BYRNE is a recent graduate of the University of Connecticut. She was born and raised in Norwalk, Connecticut and currently lives in Chicago, Illinois, where she teaches and writes.

ÍO WUERICH is an Argentinian illustrator who lives in Spain. She was born within a family full of artists, so she has always felt the freedom of doing what she loves. Her personal challenge is to draw something every single day so she can keep on learning.

JIM STILL-PEPPER's "real job" is diverse—he is a therapist working with at-risk families. He also creates living art as a public thinker throughout the country.

SAMO CREATIVE is a creative agency based in Brazil and formed by three creative minds. We are focused on strategy, content production, and audiovisual activities aimed at generating cultural impact. We are black and lgbtqi + people whose vision is to express that all bodies, speeches, and places produce and consume art. Find us online (@samo.creative).

KELSEY M. EVANS is a young artist and designer from Salt Lake City. She is inspired by the natural world and surrounds herself with plants, music, and animals. Kelsey likes to combine color and create texture in her work as a way to express emotion, movement, and spirit. In the past, Kelsey has illustrated multiple books including a series used to teach women's health with the non-profit group Healthy Am I. She is drawn to projects that focus on making the world better and hopes to continue creating designs and illustrations for meaningful causes. Find her on Instagram (@ kelseymariestudio) or at a local artisan market around Austin, TX.

ANDREW WHITE is a cartoonist interested in the interaction between abstraction, poetry, and narrative. Since 2018, he has self-published an annual comic, *Yearly*, that he hopes to continue making until he dies. Other recent work includes *Ways to Survive in the Wilderness,* a comic about grief and hope during the anthropocene, and *Letters I'll Send Tomorrow,* a collection of short stories. See more online (whitecomics.co).

KIMBALL ANDERSON makes comics for people who fell off of the conveyor belt of life. Since they were young, they've been disabled by chronic illness, and much of their work explores the ignored, quiet spaces along the periphery that people fall into. Their work has appeared in journals and anthologies like *Anomaly, Ink Brick*, and *How to Wait.* You can find more of their comics online (outside-life.com).

CASEY JO STOHRER is an artist and musician living in Nashville, TN. Her writings and comics have appeared in *The Lincoln Review, Spiralbound on Medium, The Poydras Review,* and local zines around town. She runs her own t-shirt and design company @localoblivion, and you can find her other work on Instagram ((@misscaseyjo).

DRIFTWOOD PRESS

NEW TITLES

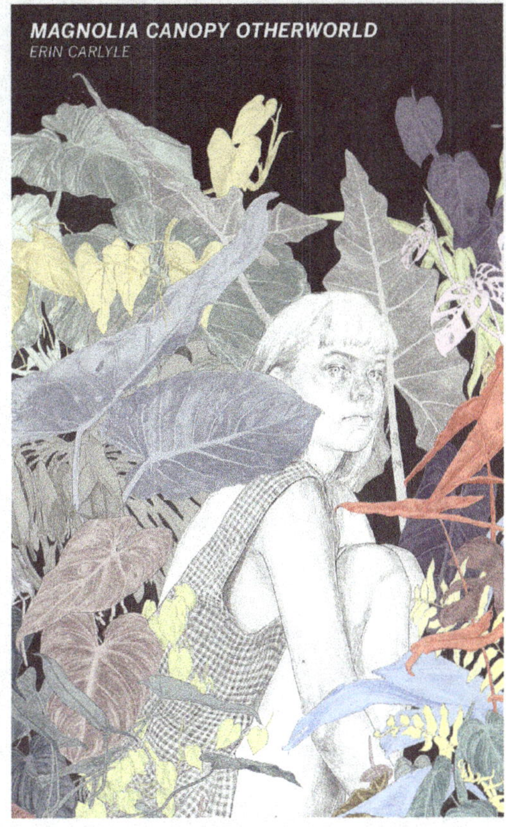

"A set of works suffused with wonder, terror, and honesty."

– Kirkus Starred Review

"*Magnolia Canopy Otherworld* explores the places that hold the muddied and forested histories of women. Sensory and sensual, Erin Carlyle's poems portray an elemental girlhood, and the fragility and publicness of a body, even in the woods. These poems are full of dangerous baptisms, teeth and hooks, gothic flora and their attendant ghosts. Carlyle's style is lush and lovely, but always tugging with its dark undertow until we feel our own animal selves rise out at the end, gasping and human again."

– Traci Brimhall,
author of *our lady of the ruins*

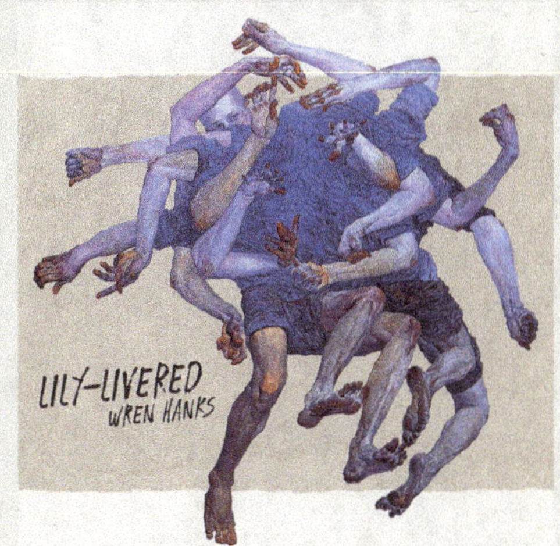

"Cyclical and dreamy, yet sinewy, Wren Hanks' *Lily-livered* is a record of the hungers—for food, for sex, for alcohol—that simultaneously tie us to and alienate us from our bodies.

– Luiza Flynn-Goodlett,
author of *Look Alive*

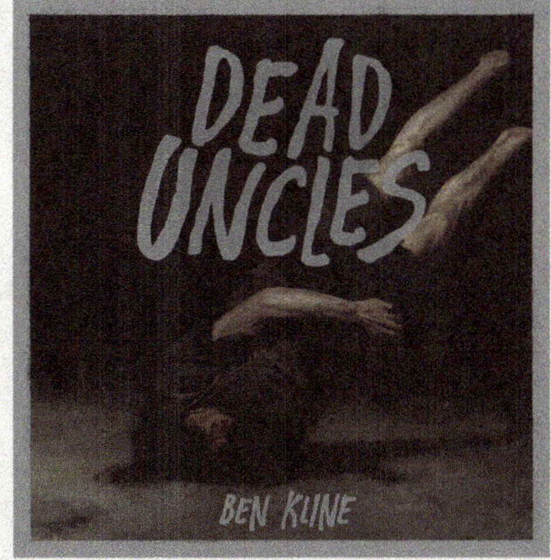

"Kline takes his foot and smears the line between the magical and the grotesque, and it is here that we discover again how to love and how to forgive."

– Taylor Byas,
author of *Bloodwarm*

www.ingramcontent.com/pod-product-compliance
Lightning Source LLC
Chambersburg PA
CBHW080401030726
47598CB00010B/2837
9781949065138